I am Mommy.

I am Mommy.

Reflections On A Powerful Choice

Susan Hughes, M.S.Ed.

Copyright © 2007 by Susan Hughes

All rights reserved.

ISBN 978-0-6151-4939-4

Printed in the United States of America

Visit my website at www.iammommy.com

For Eric and Gary – my answered prayers.

God could not be everywhere and therefore he made mothers.
  - OLD PROVERB

Contents

Introduction	1
It Wasn't Always This Way	3
The Big Decision	15
Redefinition	28
Being There	41
Choices	55
Happy Sounds	68
With Great Power Comes Great Responsibility	78
Building Character	96
The Sponge	119
School Days	131
The Question	143
About the Author	149

Introduction

The hand that rocks the cradle is the hand that rules the world.
              - WILLIAM ROSS WALLACE

I've always loved to write. This is the first time in my life that I really feel like I have something significant to write about, though. You see, I want to tell the world about the dramatic changes that have occurred in my life since giving birth to my son. "Big surprise," you may be thinking. No, I knew that my life would change, but what I didn't expect was that it would become so much better. Not small better, either. I'm talking BIG better. And this came as such a pleasant surprise to me that I felt I had to tell my story. Maybe my story parallels your story or maybe my story won't make any sense to you whatsoever! In any case, I want to share how my transformation from "manager" to "Mommy" caught me completely off-guard, swept me off my feet and took my breath away.

From my ultimate acknowledgment of the incredible speed of time to the significance of the accidental discoveries I made by simply "being there" for my son, I share with you parts of my own journey of self-discovery that I believe to be critically important to us and to the future of our world.

Being a mom has taught me the true meaning of commitment and the true meaning of unconditional love, and has given me a purpose in life that I have come to regard as more important than any other. It is my hope to inspire moms and moms-to-be to fully embrace their most important reason to be – motherhood. And for those moms who are torn between their kids and other priorities, I am hoping to provide a fresh perspective so that they are able to dig deep within themselves and realize that choosing to be "Mommy," above all else, is the most powerful choice in the world!

- Susan Hughes

~ 1 ~
It Wasn't Always This Way

The universe is change; our life is what our thoughts make of it.
- MARCUS AURELIUS ANTONINUS

A book about being a mommy? Me? Who would've thought?! Not only was I never really sure that I ever *wanted* to be a mom, but I certainly didn't think that I'd absolutely love being a mom if it happened! Well, I do love being a mom. And since I have come full circle in so many ways, I believe that I have a story that just may be worth telling.

"The old days" - surely you've heard about them. You know, they're those days that were much better than now. Not as much crime, not much in the way of technology, and the kids dressed better. Personally, I think it must have been a lot easier to be a woman in "the old days." Choices were made for us (What am I saying? We had no choices!). We knew what was expected of us right from the start and we didn't know what we were missing, if anything. There was none of this two-income family nonsense. That would have been blasphemous! Little Johnny or Janey with the label "latch-key-kid"? If there were a Child Services back then, they certainly would've come calling!

These days we women are programmed much differently than we were in our mother's or grandmother's time. Far fewer of us actually go from our childhood homes right into our husband's home or from high school right into motherhood, relishing the title of "homemaker" all the while. Today we women pride ourselves in our multi-tasking ability, striving to be all things to all people as wife, mother, employee … and not necessarily in that order. As young women growing up, we prepare ourselves for various careers outside of the home. Knowing that we must support ourselves once we leave our parents' home (and we *want* to leave our parents' home), we become employed as soon as necessary or possible, whichever comes first, and establish goals that are more under our control than, say, being swept away by Mr. Right before the first month's rent comes due. The reality is that most of us are not in the financial position to drop everything and wait for a man to come along and support us. Not only that, but not every woman wants that scenario anyway. Sure, she may welcome the companionship of a man, but don't expect her to drop her career goals and ambitions at first sight of him. After all, she may very well bring home more bacon than he does!

I, too, followed the modern route described above. And, although this book is not intended to be an autobiography, I will go into some detail describing my "route." It is, after all, how I got from there to here. Maybe my route parallels yours. Maybe it doesn't. Worst case scenario, though, you'll probably notice some similarities between the two of us.

Anyhow, getting back on track, as a young woman I was so busy with a bunch of different interests and goals that I never really got into that "gotta find a man and have a baby" mode. I guess my biological clock wasn't ticking loud enough for me to hear it, or maybe it was and I just ignored it. I've always enjoyed children, although I'll admit that I've never been one to oogle over every baby I see. Enjoying them was one thing. Giving birth to them was another thing altogether. Honestly, I was scared out of my mind about childbirth and therefore was not in any rush to experience it. I suppose that pretty much explains my biological clock silencer.

The strange thing was, through the years, no matter how scared I was of childbirth or no matter how uncertain I was about the whole mothering experience, in the back of my mind I always felt sort of an obligation to have a child or two. It was kind of a gut feeling. I don't know why, exactly. Maybe it was a fear of potential regret for not having kids? I think that's probably it. Or maybe it was just raw intuition. Perhaps I knew, deep down (very deep down, mind you), that my life would be better with kids than without, although I wasn't sure of this at all at the conscious level. No matter. One thing that this unexplainable feeling did not hinder was my progress in preparing for a career. I had to keep the ball rolling to make sure the bills would always be paid!

First, I went to college, during which time I dabbled in a variety of subjects. Although my interests and career preferences seemed to change with the wind, I was always fascinated (and challenged) by the human psyche. I knew that the sky was the limit for me in this area. After all, I had a family bursting at the seams with potential subjects for a master's thesis, not to mention a doctoral dissertation, in Psychology. I couldn't let this opportunity pass me by. Finally, my interest in psychology, coupled with my love of academia, led me to pursue a career in counseling within a college or university setting. I studied hard, stayed focused, and actually went as far as getting my Master's Degree. Then the job search began. Still no relationship, but it didn't really matter to me. Anyway, it's not like I could sit around and wait. Life kept moving; so did I.

Money became an issue, as expected, following the initial few months of my job search. I'll admit to never thinking that there would be an "initial" few months of a job search. After all, if I was competent, a job search should last no more than a month or two, right? Hmmm. Perhaps I was just getting into the job market at a bad time - too many graduates, not enough jobs, or something like that. Keeping the faith that I was, indeed, competent but in need of some help, I moved back to my hometown and continued my employment search less expensively – living with my parents and working part-time for my dad and my grandparents. I had already spent a few summers helping out part-time in their 30-year-old manufacturing business, so I had a comfort level there. It certainly seemed like the best way to tackle the challenges of my situation.

Well, my job search continued for about three more months until I decided to take on a full-time position in the family business. How about that for a 180 degree turn? I couldn't help it. It's not in me to be patient, especially when I am feeling so dependent and helpless to control my destiny. I mean, it only took a few rejections until I assumed that I must not be cut out for the whole interview thing. Basically, I made an impulsive decision out of utter frustration and the need to feel independent (and competent) once more. Actually, it really wasn't a bad change of plans. It probably was linked to some sort of quarter-life crisis. A quarter of my life was over and I wanted something to show for it – specifically, a job.

Doesn't it sometimes seem like it's all about money? Life was moving at the speed of sound, like it does for everyone after about the age of 20. In the midst of life's transitions, romance and family were not quite making it onto my list of short-term goals. Speaking of goals, can we talk about them for a minute?

I always set goals. The goals may change more often than not, but I work diligently toward each one I set until it changes. I've heard the words "obsessive-compulsive" used about me in my presence, but I beg to differ. Everybody needs goals, if for no other reason than to have a sense of purpose. If I reach a goal, I'm happy. It used to be that if I didn't reach a goal, I'd crumble. It wasn't until recently that I realized the lessons learned from merely setting a goal and pursuing it, are invaluable, whether or not I ever reach that goal. It is human nature to want to win the game, but the work or play involved has to be enjoyable to make victory worth pursuing in the first place. That being said, my goal changed in one fell swoop – no longer destined to become a college counselor, I pursued something vastly similar, yet vastly different - human resources. Of course, I threw my heart and soul into my new pursuit immediately. That is, until my heart became preoccupied.

The relationship: it's what I think I've been waiting for, but I'm not really sure. Is it a good thing or a bad thing? Next, the marriage. I'm not able to focus solely on my job anymore. It gives me something, beyond work, to look forward to. Now I *really* shouldn't work the long hours that I've *been* working. But how will I get everything done?

Thankfully my internal conflict, painful as it was, didn't have the chance to reach epic proportions. Shortly after I got married, I bought a dog and then got divorced. That last sentence may have you thinking that the dog played some devastating role in the demise of the marriage, but I assure you that was not the case. The marriage came and went in what seemed like the blink of an eye, but what actually amounted to a couple of years. Despite its lack of longevity, the experience taught me many lessons, the most significant having to do with patience. You see, during the very short honeymoon stage of the marriage, I began to think about the possibility and timing of having children. Had I insisted upon being my typically impatient self, I may not have seen the writing on the wall prior to getting terribly serious about that possibility. Nevertheless, when all was said and done, becoming a mom ceased to be an issue at that point in time due to circumstances fifty-percent beyond my control.

I never thought *I* would be A DIVORCED WOMAN. I mean, now I would have to fill in that little circle next to "DIVORCED" under the Marital Status section of government forms - not something that I would ever have expected. But who does? I mean, it would be pretty ridiculous to go through with a marriage if you didn't think it would last. I'm not being naïve. I'm sure this happens. Just because it happens doesn't mean it's not completely sick. I went into my marriage knowing that it would last. I was wrong. Oh well, time to move on. Quickly.

Divorce is one of those modern day issues that can potentially work against a woman's biological clock. We have to take the good with the bad though. With financial independence, and perhaps a slightly more complex emotional independence, a woman has the freedom to say *"I can live without you,"* but we still haven't harnessed the power to turn back time. And time certainly doesn't adjust itself to allow us to pursue our career, go through a few breakups, and finally have a few kids all prior to the onset of night sweats. The reality is that if we snooze, we lose.

So you see if I had been obsessed with childbearing when I was younger, there's no doubt that I would have been a psychological mess after my failed first marriage and a subsequent three tedious years of dating. By then I was 29 ½, an age that I once would have considered old but no longer do. Perhaps I didn't panic because my life was filled with career, friends and the option of being alone. I was free to be myself and I had the time and desire to take care of me. In fact, I became a loner, which was ironic for someone who had been petrified of being alone just a few short years earlier. Work saved me from becoming a complete recluse, because it suddenly became all-consuming, which I could have sworn it already was. My grandparents, the owners of the business, passed away suddenly. So, with barely two years in the family business under my belt, I was catapulted into a lead, and once again different, role involving the financial management of the company. Essentially, my dad and I were both forced to dive in and learn corporate accounting from the ground up.

Did I mention that I don't like change? And I didn't like accounting either. Of course, I really didn't know that I didn't like accounting because I had never experienced accounting. Balancing my checkbook was all the accounting I had ever been able to muster. One thing I *do* love is a challenge and, at the time, I was up for one, given that I had no family or significant-other responsibilities. So I immersed myself in trying to help keep the family business afloat.

Despite my immersion, I eventually began to think twice about my loner persona. I hated to admit it, but the whole single career woman thing was beginning to get old. I knew it was bad when I actually DIDN'T throw away an advertisement I received in the mail for a special deal from a popular national dating service. Yes, I questioned my own sanity. "Me ... join a dating service? Yeah right." Then came the life-changing (I didn't realize it then) power walk with my mother. We happened to run into a woman whom my mother had known for quite some time but hadn't seen in a while. It turned out that the woman had lost her husband to a serious illness a couple of years earlier. She was torn up about her loss, feeling as though she would never love again. After a period of serious depression, she decided to consider the recommendation of a close friend: to join a local dating service. Well, not only did she join, but this woman had nothing but wonderful things to tell me and Mom about her experience. The best part was that she ended up meeting and falling in love with a man who she ultimately married. I listened intently as she explained the situation. Was this chance meeting an omen? It really seemed much too coincidental not to be *some* sort of meaningful sign, although I couldn't be certain. The only thing I knew for sure was that my gut was telling me that I should call the number on the dating service ad. My decision was made.

This decision was easy to make because it was based on a gut feeling. On the flip side, oh how I feared to be labeled "desperate," a word that I was guilty of slapping onto people who read the personal ads in the paper, let alone those poor souls who spent money to find a boyfriend. Not only that, but the whole dating service concept was relatively new at that time, and seemingly was met with mixed public reaction. Once word of my brilliant new idea got out within my little microcosm of society, it was met with reactions heavily weighted towards concern. I will never forget the initial looks I got from friends and family after explaining the level to which I was about to sink socially. Still, I felt like I was on the right track, despite the sticker shock of my initial consultation at *Dating Service Headquarters*. After that experience, I felt comfortable with the assumption that nobody in their right mind would pay that kind of money unless they were serious about finding a relationship. The only other option that I could think of that could lead me to the man of my dreams, albeit not the most creative idea, was weekend barhopping. Somehow that just didn't strike me as being any better, though, so I decided to pass on that option. Seemingly, the dating service was my best shot. I drained my savings account, committed to a one-year membership, and dove in head first.

Ready, set, go! I had exactly one year to find my soul mate and I was not going to waste a minute of that time. The clock was ticking and this was no small investment financially *or* emotionally. I got right to work doing all of the necessary research: reading men's descriptions of themselves, looking at their pictures and watching their videos - not necessarily in that order! Of course, each step in the research process served to narrow my list of potential dates, and once the list was down to four or five, the service would mail a notification of my interest to each of those "finalists" while I just sat back and waited. On the flip side, men went through the same process, and, if one was interested in me, I would receive a postcard in the mail with all of the necessary information so that I could respond with interest or not. The process was time-consuming, but easy. Even when you are in a room with videotapes of available men from floor to ceiling, however, it doesn't mean that Mr. Right is one of them. Unfortunately, twelve months and twenty or so dates later, I had gotten nowhere. It seemed that every date was an exact duplicate of the last, only the name was different, as was the restaurant.

    I was bummed. I had pretty much thrown in the towel, conceded my loss. I had only a couple of weeks left in my membership and I certainly was not going to renew for another year, or I'd have absolutely no money to leave my children when I die. The unfortunate reality was that, unless I renewed for another year, I probably wouldn't have any children to leave money to anyway! Then, the unthinkable happened. With a little under a week to go as a bonafide dating service member, I received a postcard from an interested man. Should I make the drive, one last time, to check him out? Given the percentages, it would probably go nowhere so why waste the gas?

But why not waste the gas? I wavered back and forth, until I finally rationalized that I had nothing to lose so I decided to make the trip. Thank God I did that. The name on that postcard was Gary and he is my husband today.

~ 2 ~

The Big Decision

Making the decision to have a child is momentous. It is to decide forever to have your heart go walking around outside your body.
- ELIZABETH STONE

What a great thing it was to have somebody to care about again. Friends and family agreed that Gary and I are two peas in a pod, destined to be together. Of course, if you're like me you're thinking that there's no way that this can be as perfect as it seems. There's got to be a glitch in there somewhere. I mean, we have the same interests, we have similar goals, and he seems to be sort of, well, unconditional with his love. Oh, and he likes to cook. Okay, to make all of you people feel better, it's not perfect. It's just real close.

Gary and I were inseparable from the beginning. So much so that I seriously thought that this man would pop the question after only two months of dating. Yeah. This man who, at very close to forty years of age had never been married. Yup, this one really seems like the type who jumps into things.

I was right about the *two*, but not about the *months*. After two wonderful *years* of dating, Gary finally asked me to marry him. I was as happy as I had ever been. And did I mention that we were also working together? A position opened up in our business and Gary filled it. Maybe that should have concerned me. Instead, it made me even happier.

It was truly a joy to come and go from the office each day with Gary. All the while, family members warned me. Friends were uncertain. How could this arrangement work out for the best? A husband and wife spending one hundred percent of their time together, not to mention all of the stressors of a family business lurking around every corner. I'll give them that last one.

It wasn't easy to keep work and home separate. In fact, the two mixed all the time, especially when the business started struggling. If only one of us had been employed by a struggling company it would have been much easier. But both of us questioning our financial security? Now that was a different animal altogether. I carried that challenge home with me each night. We talked about it over drinks. We talked about it over dinner. We talked and talked, I suppose just to air our frustrations, because it's not like we were going to change anything. I mean, we were committed. To each other and to the business.

What's this got to do with parenting? Nothing. That is exactly my point. There was no time to even think about having a baby. No time to even have an inkling. No time to prepare. Work continued to be all-consuming and we weren't exactly bursting with financial security, which is slightly helpful when starting a family. The only security we had was each other. That sure sounds romantic. To think that, after all of the trial and error, I actually found somebody who loves me, no matter what, and who I trust implicitly. Wow, even more romantic! A friend and more, proven daily with love, support and respect. Had I refused to acknowledge all of these tear-jerky idealisms, I could have prevented *it*. But no. Suddenly, from out of the blue, at arguably the worst possible time, I was hit by "the pang!"

The "pang" - a woman's intense need for …. something. The "pang" can refer to any number of instinctive "I must have now's," but for me, at that very moment, it specifically meant "kids." Was there common sense hidden in the deep recesses of my mind? Obviously not. But, although it's true that some things in our life were quite a mess, other things in our life were really good. No matter what the reasoning, or lack thereof, once the "pang" hit me I couldn't ignore it. No, it was here to stay and it told me that it was time to start a family. And, since I clearly needed the consent of one other person, specifically Gary, prior to following through with this sudden need, I figured that I should discuss it with him.

I contemplated opening two nice bottles of wine that evening; one for Gary and the other for .... Gary. This was, after all, the first time the kid subject had come up since we were married. Way back while we were dating, Gary communicated quite openly that he would be okay with or without kids, which basically put the onus on me to ultimately decide what I wanted. If I decided to be a mom, then he'd enthusiastically become a dad. If I chose not to be a mom, he'd enthusiastically continue to be my husband. Don't get me wrong, it was very nice of him to put this decision in my lap, but given that he was split 50/50, I felt incredible pressure to accurately read the future for both of us. Nevertheless, at least we discussed all of our possibilities and concerns in great detail before tying the knot.

Of course we didn't realize at that time that the potential concerns that we discussed before we got married paled in comparison to the concerns that I was sure we would discuss now. I mean, the huge lifestyle changes that we used to worry about - like not being able to eat out at our favorite restaurant after work each night - now didn't seem so huge. Now we'd probably discuss how we would feed our children if we both lost our jobs. Even without the financial stress, there's no doubt that, at 41 and 32 respective years of age, Gary and I had gotten used to how things had been for the many years already spent in adulthood. So the question: "why change a good thing?" seemed to be very valid.

"Not always right but never in doubt." Those words come from a magnet given to me by one of my very best friends ever. What she knew about me then and what is still true of me today is that I almost always go with my gut. The "not always right" part certainly speaks the truth, but no matter, I usually listen to what I hear from deep inside myself and then go with it. And this was one of those feelings that I couldn't explain but had to go with. For some reason, though, Gary didn't quite understand the timing of my new need. And it probably wasn't the best idea to admit to him that I didn't understand either. It was just my luck that the wine didn't seem to cast its usual spell on him that night, so he wasn't exactly content with my lack of explanation. Time was ticking, though, so we had to reach some sort of agreement on this. In fact, since my pang first hit I swore that every clock in the house was amplified. Ticking. Everywhere.

Finally I was able to help Gary rationalize that time was on our side. By the time we actually became pregnant, the business would most likely be stable again. We actually thought it would take a pretty long time to get pregnant. After all, quite a few couples we knew tried for months, even years, and some even had to go the fertility route. Clearly, we could make the decision to go ahead with a family, but it wouldn't really affect our lifestyle or be an issue for quite some time. For that reason, we chose not to discuss our procreation plans with anyone else at that point.

Getting pregnant on the first try wasn't something that either of us considered to be a possibility. So when that very thing occurred I was in a state of mind which I'll loosely refer to as "shock." It has since prevented me from adequately recalling, let alone describing, my initial feelings when the pregnancy test read positive. I do recall happiness at some level, however I'm not sure that it was for the "right" reasons. I was supposed to feel happy. If I didn't feel happy, what would that mean? There was no way that I couldn't be happy. This could even be a contrived recollection, for all I know. To recall disappointment would be unacceptable and I would definitely opt to hide that away in my subconscious for fear of substantial backlash.

Whatever my initial feelings actually were, one thing was for sure: I made the decision to have a baby and now I would be happy with that decision, no matter what level of happiness that was. That being said, some other, more easily recalled feelings did pop up at the time. For one, I felt very lucky to have conceived so quickly, knowing the emotionally- and physically-painful processes some couples endure to have children. I also recall fear being strongly intermingled amongst feelings of luck and real or contrived happiness. I was scared to death. For some reason, the "never in doubt" part of my magnet wasn't holding up under these conditions. I doubted we had made the right decision, I doubted whether I could handle childbirth, and I doubted that I was ready for a lifetime of huge responsibility for another human life. Well, it really was too late to turn back.

Wouldn't it be cool if there was a way to experience the feelings that accompany a positive pregnancy test prior to the actual real thing? I think this sort of invention would alleviate all of the fears of the unknown so that when couples are faced with actual pregnancy, they are able to concentrate on the excitement and joy of a new life. On the flip side it would confirm, before it's too late, that certain people simply shouldn't become parents. No matter, I doubt there would be much uncertainty on either side of the fence after a sort of "test run." Unfortunately, technology has yet to enable us to test parenthood prior to the real thing. So, for many of us, at least for me, the fear and uncertainty undermined some of the positive feelings, like excitement and joy, through pregnancy and beyond.

Oh well. Back to the fearsome reality of multi-tasking, newly discovered pregnancy and my job. One thing that helped me get through the initial shock of our upcoming big change was my belief in the importance of planning. I think that I am capable of achieving anything as long as I plan to achieve. Well, my belief was put to the test this time around, that's for sure. I needed a plan … immediately. So, before announcing my pregnancy to my boss, a.k.a. my father, I came up with a written plan describing how I would continue to manage all of my current responsibilities with one small additional responsibility – the child.

Initially following my major announcement, I watched my father's color go from pink to white. I waited. Finally, as Dad regained his original color, I presented him with my plan. I told him that, on one hand, I was certain that I *could* just stop working and concentrate only on my new baby, but I really didn't have to do that. No, I believed strongly that I could do both, and not let anyone down. I would have the best of both worlds – no major lifestyle adjustments. That's right, no major lifestyle adjustments. Um hmmm. I would find a way to make the situation work for everyone. My dad agreed. I was thrilled. Now at least a few things could stay the same.

As soon as we were certain that everyone was okay with my plan of continuing to work while taking care of our child, Gary and I began to discuss the limitations of our current home. Up to that point, we had lived in the house that Gary had owned for many years. It was a small cape cod, not really of adequate size for all of our stuff, let alone the stuff that was going to accompany the newest member of our family. The downside was that moving into a larger place would completely eliminate my option of being a full-time stay-at-home mom. For financial reasons, I would have no choice but to continue to work for the family business. Truthfully, at the time, I had absolutely no doubt that, not only was I doing the right thing by working *and* caring for our child, but I also was certain that I would have no problem doing it that way. Had I not had the ability to take my baby to work with me and/or work out of my house, we would've stayed where we were. Neither of us considered daycare to be an option.

Speaking of daycare, this was the one subject in regard to modern motherhood that I had carefully thought out over the course of many years. For some reason I always felt strongly that it wouldn't be right for me to work outside the home, at least until my children were in school full-time. I don't know what experience, if any, led me to this conclusion. Perhaps my mother's role as stay-at-home-mom and homemaker made an impression on me. She was always there for me as I was growing up, and as a result, I felt cared for and secure - the same feeling that I wanted my children to experience. I suppose that's why I saw myself in the same role.

At that point in time, I felt very lucky to be able to have the best of both worlds, so to speak. It seemed like it would be the perfect situation. I would be at my son's beck and call every moment of every day and I could also get my work done. Seemingly there were no negatives. Personally, I don't think my common sense was operating on all cylinders. I think I was still in shock.

I did not enjoy pregnancy. This precursor to parenthood left me questioning our decision to have kids more than ever before. Plagued with nausea during months one through three, I longed for Month Four to arrive. Once Month Four was here, testing/screening anxiety set in and did not end until childbirth. The doctors ran my unborn baby and me through so many tests that it was enough to drive me crazy, especially considering that I suffer from an acute case of "test result phobia" to begin with - always imagining the worst throughout what seems like an endless wait for the results.

The most, I mean *only*, exciting test of the entire battery was the ultrasound that revealed our baby's gender. That was when it hit me. That was when being a parent became very real. Once Gary and I found out that "it" was a "he", the child was as good as born to us. At least we acted like he was already born. If it's true that a baby can learn while it is still in the womb, then our baby should have been Einstein. We immediately named him "Eric" and began to converse with him, ask him questions, read him stories and "create" his personality in our imaginations. He became a very real member of our family many months before he actually breathed the air of this world. He was a very cool unborn child, by the way. After all, he had a good sense of humor, enjoyed discussing anything that we wanted to discuss, and he held all of our same opinions. You can't ask for much more than that from a fetus, can you?

Thankfully, we passed the rest of the tests through the final months of pregnancy and moved on to one final issue: Eric's position. Yes, he was actually right-side-up in the womb, or "breech" as they call it, not upside down as preferred. I actually figured that he must be pretty smart to want to be right-side up in there, but apparently that position is too risky for natural childbirth so, if he remained like that, I'd have to get a cesarean section. Yikes.

Major surgery. The doctor assured us that there was still a good chance that he would turn during the last month, as most babies do. Not Eric. No way. He didn't want to have to get all squished and squashed on the way out. No, he wanted to be lifted out gently, even though a c-section would cause Mommy about two additional weeks of discomfort and the inability to ever wear a bikini again. (Did I say again? Ha!) In all seriousness though, the c-section possibility didn't bother me. I didn't have a violent urge to have a natural childbirth anyway. Nope. Truth be told, I really considered it to be a Godsend that my little guy refused to correctly reposition himself in the last month. Remember, I'm plan-oriented (don't even think of the words "control freak") so, needless to say, I was not the least bit excited about a surprise water breakage and mad rush to the hospital in the middle of the night. Instead, because of Eric's stubbornness, we were able to calmly proceed to the hospital for his "birth appointment." No labor pains or anything. I was definitely okay with that!

We got to the hospital at 9:00 am on Eric's birthday. I wasn't in labor, or so I thought, but the nice nurses informed me that the machines to which I was hooked were indeed telling them that I *was* in labor. Well, who am I to argue with technology, but I will say that if labor felt like that I don't think natural childbirth would've been a problem. Actually, I'm sure that I was in a numb sort of mode at that point, hence the lack of pain.

I quickly got out of numb mode, however, when the nurses began to prep me for surgery. One of the nurses was finding it nearly impossible to locate a vein into which she could successfully stick the I.V. She must have been a positive thinker because she certainly didn't give up! Finally, thankfully, another nurse came to my rescue and got the needle in where it was supposed to be.

Sweaty and anxious from the I.V. trauma, I really needed something to relax me. A glass of wine was out of the question, but I was happy to find out that relaxation was the whole point of the I.V. in the first place. It began to drip and I began to calm down. The next thing I knew, I was being wheeled down to the operating room.

Gary was given a set of "scrubs" to change into before meeting us down in the operating room, since he had decided to brave the blood and guts portion of this unfolding drama (or comedy). I was glad that he would be with me. There was no doubt that I was very relaxed, but I wouldn't be asleep for the c-section, which presented a slight concern for me, especially when I realized, as we entered the operating room, that the only thing separating me from my soon-to-be gaping abdominal cavity was a small curtain hanging directly above my chest. Gary had the option of sitting down, in essence hiding, behind the curtain or standing up to watch the entire procedure. To my surprise, he chose to watch. I, on the other hand, felt more comfortable behind the curtain.

As soon as my doctor and his assistant arrived, they began to talk about golf. Clearly they must watch primetime medical dramas, I thought, because that's what surgeons do on TV. I really was hoping that they would concentrate on what they were doing, but I figured that they did this successfully so many times before that they could talk about whatever they wanted to.

There I was, gutted and forlorn. Numb from the waist down and the eyebrows up. Not knowing what to expect but aware that, at some point amidst the pulling and tugging going on just behind the curtain, a small child would appear with a coating of slime and blood. Not a very pretty sight, I was sure.

~ 3 ~

Redefinition

Suddenly she was here. And I was no longer pregnant; I was a mother. I never believed in miracles before.

- ELLEN GREENE

Baam! In the midst of blood and guts, the child is born. The miracle of birth. A cesarean birth; as previously assumed, not a pretty sight, but miraculous nonetheless. To this day, Gary's clearest memory of the birth experience was when the doctor, just after delivery, held the very bloody, slimy Eric close to me and I exclaimed "he's so adorable!" Had my life just been redefined? Obviously. If I could think that this tiny human being laced with mangy stuff was "adorable," then some sort of redefinition or revelation must have occurred. Suddenly everything became quite clear. From this point on, my contribution to the world would be through my son. For a split second, all fear and anxiety disappeared while I contemplated that thought. What had just happened was, indeed, a gift from God. And God's gift to me will be my gift to the future.

I finally snapped out of my deep meditation, only to find Eric still in need of a bath. "If this kid is going to be my gift to the future, somebody better make him presentable," I thought. The nurses were definitely thinking the same thing I was, because just then they whisked him away for a good cleaning. And I didn't even get to hold him. They had plans for me, though. While Eric was being cleaned up I had to pay a visit to the recovery room for an hour or so until my legs regained feeling. Thankfully, at the time, it never occurred to me to doubt whether or not they actually ever *would* regain feeling. The intravenous medication seemed to play a role in drastically reducing the barrage of "what-ifs" that typically shot through my mind. Come to think of it, the intravenous medication also seemed to play a role in erasing most of my memories of the Recovery Room. I hardly remember anything about being there. Except for the clock, that is. It seemed like a rather giant clock. The hands moved ever so slowly as I kept watching it and waiting. Thoughts raced in and out of my head while I waited to feel something, anything, having to do with my legs. Thoughts like "I'm a mommy. Me. Wow." played over and over again in my head until finally, suddenly, I felt a tingling. And once it started, it didn't waste any time moving from my toes to my hips, allowing me to feel normal again from the waist down. In fact, before I knew it a team of nurses pushed me out of the Recovery Room into the elevator and up to a very cheery, brightly-colored room on the maternity floor. The meds must have worn off by then, because my nerves started their all too familiar dance. I was excited but nervous for the arrival of the cleaned up, presentable version of my son.

Thankfully, before my nerves could gain complete control of my psyche, Gary and my mom showed up to check on me and give me the latest report on Eric. Excellent. He weighed in at just under eight pounds, had all of his fingers and toes (and a lot of hair) and was otherwise healthy. Thank God. He just had to come up to the right temperature, and then a nurse would bring him to me. The right temperature? I felt my heart jump. What did that mean? Gary and Mom, both realizing my heightened state of anxiety, assured me that there was nothing to be concerned about. Eric was chilly and he needed some warmth. No big deal. I knew they would tell me the truth. Calm down Sue.

Okay, now that we were past those little details, I could focus on myself again. Nobody had to know that I was focusing on myself, either. No, I could let my mind travel on a journey of negativity, and nobody had to know. I'M A PARENT!! What will I do with my baby? How will I hold him? Will I be a good mom? I tried, with very limited success, to stop all of these thoughts, but they had taken over. I couldn't let anyone know that I was losing it mentally. The funny part is that, looking back, I realize that the whole parent thing really hadn't even hit me yet. I had yet to hold my son, let alone really understand what motherhood was all about.

In the midst of my secret mental panic, there was a knock at the door. One of the nurses came in holding Eric. My panic intensified, and I think the nurse could tell, although nobody else seemed aware. I had my happy face on to show the world that I was joyfully prepared to face this challenge. My mind continued to race: "Yes! I am a mommy! I can handle everything from this point on! Out of my way, nurse! Give me my son!" Unfortunately, the nurse could see through any bravado that I thought I was conveying. The extremely slow, careful manner in which she handed Eric over to me really tipped me off. She was clearly allowing me to get a grip (literally and figuratively) before she transferred one hundred percent of his seven plus pounds to my arms. This was something that would definitely take some getting used to. He was so tiny! Yet he had all the little fingers and toes and the little nose and little mouth …. he was breathing …. and had such tiny lips and … yes … I was genuinely overwhelmed by the miracle of his birth. This little bundle was completely dependent on us now. Gary and I must make sure he has a happy life … or at least give him the best possible chance at it.

Gary and Mom and I took turns holding Eric. I couldn't stop staring at him. I felt protective of him. I felt like he was my responsibility. How strange it felt. We had a bond, but I don't know how it had happened. How do you share a bond with somebody you don't even know?

After about an hour of holding, Eric was ready for a nap. Truth be told, so was I. My abdomen did not let me forget that it had a big incision across it. One of the negatives of cesarean birth, I suppose, but one that I could live with for a short time. The doctor had told me that I'd be back to normal in two weeks, and I wanted to believe him, but I couldn't imagine that my pain could possibly subside in such a short time. What I felt was not a mere "ache," mind you, but more like the pain after being cut with a knife. Wait. I <u>was</u> cut with a knife. Anyhow, the nurse came back for Eric, and I gladly handed him over. Had I not been in pain, I could have held him and stared at him all day. But I had limitations that I, and my loved ones, willingly acknowledged. So, knowing I was struggling a bit, Mom and Gary went on their way, leaving me to get some sleep before Eric's next visit.

And sleep I did. When I awoke, Gary was back and the nurse was ready to bring Eric back for a feeding. No problem. I felt confident about feeding him. I was just weak on every other aspect of mothering!

Who knows, maybe eventually we would be okay parents. After all, we were gaining confidence as we pondered the day's events, ignorant to the fact that we would falter in our even deeper exploration of basic baby care later that night. It would be then, during our initial solo attempt to change Eric's diaper, that our newbie parental status would become especially evident.

Yes, that first diaper change clocked in at a whopping 60 minutes. It was like we were changing the diaper of a giant eggshell. All I knew was that, if it continued to be that difficult, I'd either have to limit Eric's food intake, which wouldn't be ethical, or I'd have him potty trained before he was a year old. I mean, at this rate, changing diapers would threaten to completely take over our existence.

If only Gary and I had realized, right from the beginning, that babies are rather durable, life would have been much easier. After all, babies couldn't be too delicate, or the human race would be extinct by now, given the clumsiness of us adults. Well, eventually we did realize this, and the result was a drastic reduction of the time and effort spent on diapering and anything else that involved handling the little guy.

The next couple of days of so-called rest and recovery in the hospital passed rather quickly even though most of my waking and sleeping hours were spent ... well... awake. Family and friends visited and Gary was with us every chance he could be. Eric and I bonded through the trials and tribulations of the breastfeeding learning curve, with the very attentive help of the nursing staff. Basically, whenever Eric was hungry, which frequently seemed to be in the middle of the night, a nurse would bring him to me and plop him on top of me. Let the feeding begin!

I was lucky. Breastfeeding worked right away. I had heard many horror stories about women not being able to get the baby to latch on and then ultimately giving up on the whole idea. The nurses commented immediately that Eric was an excellent "rooter." Thank you. "What the heck is a 'rooter'?" I eventually wondered aloud. Well, apparently babies have an instinct that tells them to search for a nipple in order to get food. They sort of shake their head back and forth till they find what they are looking for. Eric definitely had this move down, because he found milk and latched on almost immediately. That's the good news.

The bad news is that I'm not good when I'm lacking sleep. I need my eight hours, at least. A mother of a newborn just doesn't get a good night's sleep (or at least what *I* consider to be a good night's sleep). And breastfeeding presents the challenge of even more extensive sleep deprivation. That is one redeeming quality about bottle-feeding your baby - just about anyone can do that for you ... i.e. nurse, husband, etc. Not so with breastfeeding, obviously. Thankfully, I survived sleep deprivation, probably because I was so pumped with adrenaline during my hospital stay from the rush of being a new mom combined with all of the unknowns and dramatic changes. Basically, my brain was operating in high gear around the clock. Sure, I was tired, but somehow I managed to function.

After three adrenaline-pumped but relatively pleasant days in the hospital, it was finally time to go home. I hoped that we had enough practice holding and changing, and changing and holding. After all, day to day reality was about to begin, without the help of a professional nursing staff. How would it feel? Did we know enough? Would my incision ever stop hurting?! Stop brain, stop!

I took a necessary, though short, break from stressing out while I struggled to get dressed in normal clothes again. This, in its own right, was a challenge. I had stretchy pants and a large, pregnancy size shirt which, normally, would've been easy to change into, however my incision severely limited my movement. I struggled through it, though.

Once Gary arrived and we were almost ready to go, the nurses finally delivered Eric to my room and informed me of the unseasonable 65 degree December warmth. So much for the nice selection of warm clothes and blankets I had prepared for my son's departure. Hmmm. What does a mom do when she thinks it will be cold outside but it is actually warm? Does she still over-dress the newborn just for protection? Or does she eliminate some layers so he can be comfortable? After soliciting some feedback from the nursing staff and from Gary, I chose the latter option. Then, as soon as Eric was wrapped up and ready to go, my hospital entourage wheeled me to the lobby where I let my mind settle down prior to facing our next challenge: the carseat.

Our performance with the carseat echoed the incompetence of the diaper-changing debacle. After close to twenty minutes of pushing and pulling, clicking and clacking, I reached the premature conclusion that it would *always* take us an hour to change the kid and then another hour to get him into his carseat to take him anywhere! Yes, the decision was made. We would spend the first year of Eric's life in the house, just to save the time and trouble. Although it did seem to take forever to finally get Eric into his carseat and, although I'm not sure we had it configured exactly right, he definitely seemed secure. With so many straps and latches how could he not be safe?

I still have vivid memories of my own carseat as a young child. It was a blue vinyl upright chair placed in the middle of the front seat, facing forward. If not for the statute of limitations, I could sue my parents. At least, through extensive time and effort, technology has benefited us in this regard. So instead of cursing the carseat, I will choose to be thankful for the carseat. Not only will it keep Eric safe, but I will soon come to find out that it will enable him to sleep soundly at times when nothing else does the trick.

Eric cried as we drove home. This was new. "Why is Eric crying? How do we make him stop? Is he sick? Is he uncomfortable?" This was an aspect of new motherhood that drove me absolutely crazy. I definitely could not deal with my baby crying. I had to make him stop. Gary seemed to be just as uncomfortable with this situation as I was. We figured out, much later of course, that crying is a normal baby thing and it's going to happen no matter how hard parents try to make it stop. Nevertheless, as new parents, we definitely could not deal with it. Just then I felt a sense of warmth and security as I thought back to my recent decision not to leave the house during Eric's first year.

"Where's the pacifier?" Gary asked.

"Is he hungry?" I followed up.

"Maybe he has gas." Gary suggested.

We didn't know. At least that first drive was a short 10-minute trek, because I think if it had been any longer, Gary and I would both have needed a therapist.

As we pulled into our driveway, my thoughts turned to how things used to be. When I left the house last, I wasn't a mommy. Now, I am a mommy. It's crazy, but I do that all the time. I guess I'm always amazed at how things can change with the blink of an eye. Again, I let out a sigh and a "wow" that Gary heard very clearly, prompting him to voice concern about my well-being. I assured him that I was fine, just a little overwhelmed by my expectations of what was to come.

In the dictionary, *to expect* means "to look forward to the probable occurrence or appearance of," or "to consider likely or certain." Expectation was a dangerous animal, especially since Gary and I were dealing with something completely new to us. We had no parenting experience of our own from which to draw, so we satisfied our curiosity on the subject by listening to other people.

Looking back, it made no sense at all to get worked up about the trials and tribulations of other people's mothering experiences, but I still did just that. I couldn't help it. For the first time ever, we were entering our home with the names "Mommy" and "Daddy." A whirlwind of what potentially was to come was blowing all around us while we continued to move forward and adjust to our new roles. But to allow our reality to be based on expectation, rather than to have our expectation be based on reality, was dumb. Sure, we sought comfort in the baby stories eagerly shared by friends and family. There were good stories. There were bad stories. There were scary stories and joyful stories. We listened to <u>all</u> of the stories. We listened and based our expectations on those stories, all the while failing to realize how different our story could be. That period of time was marked by much wasted apprehension and unnecessary stress.

My first of many incorrect expectations was that I would see Eric for the first time and immediately have this unbelievable attachment to him. Don't get me wrong, as I mentioned before, I felt a sort of instinctive bond with him right away, but it wasn't of the intensity that I expected. I'm talking about that "what would I ever do if I lost him" feeling that I always had when I loved someone deeply. This initial lack of intensity scared me. When I get scared, the wacko thoughts start rolling. "Should I have become a mother? Am I ever going to love this child the way a mother *should* love her children? Maybe this whole parenting thing was just a bad idea!"

Many magazine articles and parenting books later, I came to realize that everyone reacts differently to being a new parent. Bonding with a new baby can take days, weeks and even months. It is different for everyone. "Hey Doctor OBGYN, that piece of information would have been *extremely* valuable!" With hormones surging and change ensuing, there was no way that I would have been able to stop and reason through my feelings at that point. Instead, I jumped on my own mental bandwagon that told me I shouldn't have become a mother. There it was again, more needless stress and anxiety that only served to remove any joy whatsoever from the situation. If I had only known, at the time, how much the depth of my love for Eric and our mutual attachment would develop and grow - well beyond what it was on that day of his birth. That knowledge would have saved me a lot of trouble.

In general, I had too much information. Too many stories from other parents, too much statistical data - including the milestones, the height and weight charts, reading and writing levels, and, of course, manuals – that were way too readily available. They all may have their place in the process of educating new parents, but I truly felt it was overkill. Too much information like that did little more than make me crazy with expectations. And expectations lead to labels, which in turn lead to reactions. Once reactions are solidified, we have self-fulfilling prophecies. If there were to be a next time, I'd definitely take the general rules and guidelines of motherhood with a grain of salt and remember that every parent is different, every child is different, and every family is different. Not much can be accurately generalized.

~ 4 ~
Being There

The commonest fallacy among women is that simply having children makes them a mother - which is as absurd as believing that having a piano makes one a musician.

- SYDNEY J. HARRIS

Expectations aside, it was time to gather up our little bundle of joy and show him his new home. Oh my. Was it my imagination, or was he suddenly asleep? This was our first lesson on the magic of car rides. As though I haven't already applauded the modern-day carseat enough, I'd like to quickly point out another benefit, besides safety, of this dramatically improved technology. Our new carseat enabled us to move Eric inside the house without waking him. Yes, the incredible detaching carseat was the answer to every parent's dream. Simply remove the seat from its base and carry it, along with its sleeping contents, to the destination of choice. Who thinks of these things? (Some guy who is now sipping a pina colada on a lovely island somewhere, no doubt.)

Once we got into the house, Eric continued to sleep in his carseat for several hours, giving Gary and me some much needed time to relax and take everything in. We flopped down on the couch ever so quietly, knowing that, from now on, times like this would be very rare. Suddenly there was snoring. Then there was none. Then, out of the blue, I heard the sound of a baby crying. "Whose baby is that?" I wondered to myself, waking slowly from what was my first and last nap in a number of years. Gary must have been experiencing similar delirium, judging by the look on his face as his head popped up off of the pillow.

"Do you want me to get him?" I detected an air of *"please say no"* in Gary's considerate offer.

"No, I'll get him. Or maybe ... well, yes, if you don't mind." I couldn't help but rethink my response as I attempted to get up off of the couch only to quickly reach the conclusion that movement was not my strong suit just yet.

Gary gently placed the crying Eric on my lap. Eric needed something just then, and I was the one who must provide it. I didn't know what "it" was, but I had to figure it out. It didn't matter that I felt pain with every movement. It didn't matter if I had other things I wanted to do. The only thing that mattered was that Eric got what he needed. That's when it hit me. From that point on, I had to "be there" for my son. Not just be *around* my son, but sincerely, enthusiastically and completely be *there* for him. It was then when I also realized the colossal responsibility that I had chosen to undertake. Usually if my mood changed or if my schedule was too filled up, I could simply adjust the order of my priorities. Not in this case. My son had to be number one on my list despite what else was happening in my world. Oh yes, this was a very important defining moment for me, but I didn't realize at the time that there were many more defining moments still to come.

Motherhood was no longer just a fantasy; it was actually time to begin the trial and error process of raising a child. He's on my lap and he's "rooting." Okay. That one's easy. He's hungry. Trust me, it wasn't always that simple though. After he ate, he cried. It could be a wet diaper or he could have a tummy ache. After a diaper change, he cried. No more wet diaper, but he could be hungry again, or it's a tummy ache. I wondered just how many tummy aches a baby could have. Clearly, the tummy ache became the default problem. Poor Eric, when I think of how many doses of baby antacid he received within his first few months of life. Not to worry though, it wasn't long until I began to figure things out. Not only did I figure things out, but I even began to formulate lots of opinions that I could willingly and all too joyfully pass on to the next mothers-to-be. I suppose what goes around comes around.

The passing of time certainly did help Gary and me, as new parents, understand Eric more and chill out a little bit. Although we continued to struggle to control our expectations, overall life began to return to normal. A new type of normal, that is. This *new normal* entailed getting half the amount of sleep I was once used to. It entailed taking care of somebody else for more hours a day than I took care of myself. And, last but not least, *normal* now meant deciphering somebody else's wants and needs by mere instinct. Much of this *new normal* was very frustrating for me, but of all the potentially negative aspects, the sleep deprivation part got to me the most.

I won't pretend that I can function well on less than a solid eight hours of sleep, because I cannot. There are many witnesses that will gladly attest to that. The good thing was that I didn't have time to focus on my lack of sleep or any of the other frustrating stuff, for that matter, because I had, in fact, committed to resuming the duties of my job immediately upon returning from the hospital. Obviously I was unable to acknowledge that I had just had major surgery. Forget the fact that I couldn't move very much or very well on my own, let alone with a baby on my hip. And Eric practically lived on my hip those first few months as we moved from room to room while I took calls, did the books, and, in the midst of all of that work-related stuff, attended to my mothering duties.

Was it a stupid decision to return to the duties of my job immediately? "Stupid" is a strong word that I prefer not to use. I'll just say that, hindsight being 20/20, quite bluntly I should have been committed for committing. During that time I definitely discovered that I had ego-oriented issues that needed addressing. For one, I thought I could do everything. In fact, it never even occurred to me that I couldn't. Of course nobody can do everything, but I was in denial, so I kept trying. That being said, having insufficient time and energy to dwell on the "what-ifs" was an invaluable benefit resulting from my ... let's call it .... *naïveté*.

I must credit the passing of time with a few more positives: in time Eric and I finally fell into a routine that worked for us and for everyone else. In time Gary and I continued to gather proof and gain confidence that our son wasn't breakable, allowing us the privilege of being increasingly calm and relaxed. Finally, and perhaps most importantly, in time my c-section healed. Actually, the healing happened exactly as the doctor told me it would – after about two weeks, the pain disappeared almost suddenly. To me, that represented the elimination of the most painful and annoying roadblock that, up to that point, prevented me from really settling into a routine that most resembled *normal* as it used to be. So, in the long run, there were plenty of positive changes to offset the frustrations, and, as I've pointed out, most of these positive changes were directly related to the passage of time.

Yes, as time went by, things seemed to get increasingly better. For this reason, at that time I was truly naïve to the downside of time's incredible speed and how, one day soon, I would give anything just to make it stand still for awhile.

Now that my temporary friend "time" had helped me make it well beyond the starting point of the mommy learning curve, or so I thought, I considered it the perfect time to prove to everyone that I could be a great mom *and* a great employee. All it would take was a little multi-tasking, so that's just what I did. I worked at my job diligently in the early morning hours, making whatever phone calls I could while Eric was engrossed in his favorite TV shows. Guilt-ridden over the highly publicized damaging effects of TV, but not aware of any viable options, I turned to PBS as a babysitter for a couple of hours each morning.

The truth is that I'll be forever thankful to PBS for their amazing children's programming. Not only was Eric entertained while I worked, but he also learned quite a bit. Perhaps it would have been better for me and for Eric had I been the one entertaining him during those early morning hours. Maybe he would have enjoyed simply being held or rocked quietly during that time. I don't know. What I do know is that it doesn't seem to me that the television hurt him. As far as learning was concerned, without a detailed lesson plan and a wide array of props, I could not have come close to giving him the information imparted by the likes of Sesame Street in such a short amount of time. And I was certain that the mainstream concern of that time - that too much TV caused obesity and atrophied muscles - didn't apply in Eric's case, since he was as active as any newborn could be for all but a couple of his waking hours.

I hold the theory that anything done in moderation, providing that it is legal and morally acceptable, is not likely to cause damage. In fact, strict limitations sometimes backfire and become the fuel for obsession. I've actually seen that happen in more than a few situations where limits were imposed on kids for television or video games, and the unexpected result was the child's insatiable need for those activities whenever the restrictions were relaxed or lifted. Eric definitely enjoyed watching his favorite shows, but, thankfully, he didn't *need* his favorite shows.

Following Eric's early morning date with Elmo and my quality time with Microsoft Excel, late morning was upon us, so playtime became the priority. Playtime with a newborn was not what I considered exciting. Realistically, what can one do if one can't support one's own head? We still found ways to have fun though. I spent a lot of time talking to Eric and he even talked back to me in his own language. Being his Mommy, I knew exactly what he was saying and, of course, it was all good. Obviously, he had already learned that if he doesn't have anything nice to say, he shouldn't say anything. In addition to our philosophical discussions, we sang songs, counted fingers and toes and just plain enjoyed each other's company until it was time for lunch.

Lunch time with an infant doesn't exactly burst with excitement either, due mostly to an obvious lack of variety. And consider yourself forewarned that "lunch time *with* an infant" is more accurately stated as "lunch time *for* an infant," since the infant is the only one getting lunch at that time. My hunger and Eric's current lack of food options didn't stop us from continuing to chat, though. We happily discussed Eric's future while he rooted and sucked until that glorious time when he fell asleep in my arms – or not.

One would think that, between the monotony of drinking only milk all the time and the tediousness of discussing his future just days after his birth, Eric would unquestionably drift off to sleep as soon as his tummy was filled. Not so. Keep in mind that there are no guarantees. Nevertheless, if it didn't happen immediately after lunch, he *would* go to sleep by early afternoon, whether he wanted to or not. By that time Eric and I were *both* in dire need of rest, though only one of us had that pleasure. For me, Eric's naptime represented the gun firing at the start of a race. As soon as his little head hit the mattress it was time for me to put the pedal to the metal. God help any local urchins, neighbors or door-to-door salespeople who happened to stop by uninvited and ring the doorbell. Eric was a great sleeper, unless someone whispered or a nearby insect accidentally dropped a crumb. Forgive my sarcasm. It's just that naptime was very frustrating for me. Most of the time, it came and went only once daily and its duration, based solely on the decibel level of the house, the neighborhood and the region, was always a surprise. If Eric awoke prematurely, all bets were off. The work that I needed to get done would remain unfinished and any portion of our routine that normally followed naptime would be destroyed because Eric, suffering from the effects of an incomplete nap, would unquestionably arise as "Angry Baby Seeking Revenge". In this regard, my nerves took a daily beating.

On the other side of the coin, a successful naptime meant a smooth and pleasant afternoon. Not only could I at least finish my most important work prior to the first signs of life from my son, but when he awoke he did so with happier-toned cries and patience atypical of an infant. At least it seemed like that. Then, after his afternoon snack, I was one hundred percent Eric's once again to play, talk or just curl up and snuggle. That was our afternoon up until dinner time.

The cool thing about our schedule was that it actually worked well. Sure, we had to tweak it here and there, but, overall, things went smoothly. Actually, as time went on, it even began to improve. Both Eric and I became more flexible and more tolerant. Eric learned to sleep through a ringing doorbell. I learned that multi-tasking was more of an art than a science. A very stressful art, but well worth the gray hair it caused. Let's face it: I was fortunate to have the opportunity to be with my son throughout the day and, at the same time, help support our family financially. Because I was (and still am) grateful for that privilege, I didn't take it for granted. I was there to notice the subtle changes in Eric and I personally witnessed each milestone. And as I said before, things were becoming easier and more familiar with the passing of each day.

Yes, we were finally at a comfortable point. That's when it happened. For the first time, I really felt like time was moving way too fast. I had to try to make it stop, or at least slow it down. I could handle things now. No need for any more familiarity, things were just fine the way they were.

Unfortunately, time doesn't stop. And it doesn't do any good for me to try to make it stop, because in the process of doing so I miss everything cool that is going on around me in the present. I finally understand that fact after wrestling with time and being defeated again and again. So, it was in our best interest for me to stop fighting time and face the next challenging stage of my multi-tasking arrangement: going in to the office to work, twice a week, with Eric in tow. This new setup would entail more telephone interruptions, more meetings, employee problems - the list goes on and on. I was certain that the routine that Eric and I had come so close to mastering was about to come to a devastating end. Surely we would have less flexibility with our play time, and naptime would be next to impossible. This time my own past experience formed my expectations.

When would I learn? I had years of experience at the office under my belt so I knew what to expect, right? The only problem was that I had never been in this *exact* situation before, so my past experience really didn't count for much. Once again I could have saved myself a lot of stress and anxiety by adopting *positive* expectations rather than negative ones, since, once again, the negative ones never came to fruition anyway. It actually turned out that everybody at the office was respectful and supportive of what I was trying so desperately to accomplish, and Eric and I were respectful and supportive back, so we were able to make our arrangement work at the expense of nobody. We were even able to stick pretty closely to our original routine, with the addition of a little bit more tolerance and flexibility for sanity's sake. Yet another lesson learned regarding the potentially time-wasting effects of expectations.

At the time, the whole concept of a mother taking her child to her office was relatively new. Don't get me wrong - I know that most women don't take their kids to work anyway, at least not all the time, even though this type of arrangement may be more accepted now than it was a few short years ago. It's probably a good thing if it's not a really popular option. It may very well be easier to work within a strict, next-to-nothing budget than to multi-task with a young child on a full-time basis. The only reason that I even attempted it was because I had that ego problem which I admitted to earlier.

Seriously though, I had only one goal in mind from the start: to be with my son as much as possible. Had I not been able to spend time with Eric each day *and* keep my job, Gary and I would have downsized so that I could be a stay-at-home mom. Ironically, I always considered myself a stay-at-home mom anyway – just with a few added responsibilities outside of the family. The setting never mattered to me because, when it got right down to it, the only important thing was that Eric and I were able to spend time together. I wanted us to have "our" life, instead of "his" life and "my" life.

Looking back, as difficult as it sometimes was, the variety that we had in our schedule actually made life pretty fun and interesting for Eric and me. Even learning life's many lessons took on a slightly different twist at the office. For instance, it was very early on that Eric learned to be respectful and patient during those times when I absolutely had to be in a meeting or on the phone. Oh sure, it was basically the same lesson he would have learned had he been at home and in need of my attention while I was in the middle of cooking dinner or cleaning. At the office, though, I didn't have the option of getting lazy with discipline since a tantrum would not only disturb me, but it would also totally disrupt a bunch of other people. Eric learned to understand and respect that. And since acting out at the office got him absolutely nowhere (except alone with me in my office with the door closed) Eric made the logical choice to behave . . . most of the time.

Once he grew to be a toddler, Eric occasionally attended meetings and became very eager to help out, even if it entailed the mere push of the "SEND" button on the fax machine. There is no doubt in my mind that his experiences at the office taught him a great deal of self-control and responsibility. That's not to say that he wouldn't have learned similar lessons at home by doing things like setting the table or waiting patiently for Mommy to finish a phone conversation with a friend. I suppose the lessons were the same, but the setting was different. I do believe, though, that his experience at the office made him much more sensitive to the ways in which his behavior affects other people. I often consider that the office represented Eric's own little microcosm of society through which he could learn and safely test what he learned. And since I was there right along with him, he, too, had the best of both worlds.

It's probably quite clear by now that my inability to stop time actually ended up being a good thing. In fact, it *all* ended up being a good thing. My ego-oriented drive first led to my stay-at-home-working-mom role, which, in turn, led to some of the most important lessons of my life. Amongst those is a lesson in what I consider to be the single most important aspect of being a mom: how to truly *be there* for my son. I learned that I <u>must</u> live in the moment. I mean, I certainly can't be here for Eric if I'm not really … well … <u>here</u>.

Whatever the terminology – living in the present or in the here and now - it all refers to truly experiencing what is happening at this very moment, rather than pondering the past or worrying about the future. This concept does not come naturally for me and was actually very foreign to me pre-Eric. In fact, I've missed so much stuff going on in the present that I should be several years younger. It's not that I haven't wanted to live in the here-and-now, because

I've certainly tried, but I've struggled. "What-ifs" have been the bane of my existence.

It wasn't until Eric was born that I truly began to comprehend the negative effects of NOT living in the moment. It's funny how certain experiences can make things clearer than they've ever been. For one, my multi-tasking was effective only when I focused on the present. With only limited chunks of time available to me, I certainly wouldn't have been able to get my work done without being in the here-and-now, and even more importantly, I could not have given Eric the undivided attention that he deserved during *our* time together. Looking ahead or looking behind was a waste of the time that was already in short supply, and doing just that had the power to rob me of precious time and memories with my son. I had no choice. In order to prevent countless regrets, I had to learn to live and think differently. It wasn't easy, but at least it wasn't too late.

~ 5 ~

Choices

Mother love is the fuel that enables a normal human being to do the impossible.
- MARION C. GARRETTY

As if I hadn't yet mastered the art of living in the moment, I was presented with one final test of my newfound mental ability – the demise of the family business. Yes, the day came when I finally confronted, in the comfort of Eric's sandbox, the fact that the struggling family business could survive no longer. There I was –barefooted and enjoying playtime with my son, fully focused on the here-and-now, when the telephone rang. My dad's somber voice at the other end of the line advised me of the half-expected, though long-denied, truth.

Despite our best effort, the business was done. Finished. For those few moments, I must admit that I abandoned the here and now to make a quick journey back to "Woulda-Coulda-Shoulda Land" and, of course, "The Land of What If." Hey, hadn't anyone heard me before?! I was okay with the way things were. I was comfortable. Things were familiar. And yes, my arrangement was working. I had known for quite some time, deep down, that this was a potential outcome, but, until this latest phone call from Dad, I was definitely in denial.

Now, my sudden acceptance of reality forced me to face yet another transition: going from partially employed to *definitely not* employed. And that was just me – Gary's change would be slightly more severe: fully employed to *definitely not* employed. Did I mention that I hate change? I'm sure that I did, but if I didn't mention it directly, I'm sure it's becoming apparent by now. My feelings were such that I had to resist a very strong urge to bury my head in the sand . . . literally. I realized that such a reaction would not be acceptable, however, as Eric may follow my lead. And although many children have probably learned this cowardly reaction in the figurative form, teaching Eric the literal act of burying his head in the sand while playing in the sandbox would be well over the top.

Going forward, I *really* couldn't help having negative expectations. I had no idea what Gary and I would do to make money, and I knew that I wouldn't have many, if any, work options that would allow me to stay home with Eric. Clearly this latest transition brought with it a variety of the most challenging tests to date, forcing me to revisit just about all of the little lessons that I thought I had mastered over the past few years. I'd be lying if I said that I passed these tests with flying colors. Quite the contrary, I'm afraid. For one, although I tried desperately to stick to my "no expectations" rule, I was having little success for the reason that I pointed out above. Then there was my long-time dedication to being-in-the-moment. If a teacher was handing out a grade for this one, mine would've been no better than a "C." Unfortunately, I couldn't stop wondering how in the world we would handle all of the changes facing us. The only activity that put me back in the moment was spending time with Eric. Otherwise I was always so far ahead of myself that it was pretty ridiculous. Then there was the single most significant question of all: Would my outspoken priority – to stay home to be with Eric – be compromised when our family could no longer afford the lifestyle to which we had become accustomed?

One thing's for sure: experiencing the uncertainty of unemployment definitely helped Gary and me get to the bottom of what we're all about. Values, priorities, patience – I found out they're all put to the test during financial desperation. And, quite honestly, I was under the mistaken impression that our beliefs about parenting had not truly been tested up to that point, which is why I had to ask myself that question at the end of the last paragraph. I assumed that, since I didn't have to make a so-called "cut-and-dried" choice between my career and my son, my convictions about being a stay-at-home mom weren't necessarily valid. I definitely talked the talk, but until I had to make a definitive choice on the matter, I didn't feel as though I was "walking the walk."

But the reality was that I had already made a definitive choice. Through my unique arrangement of working from home and raising Eric, I was, in fact, honoring the commitment that Gary and I made long before Eric breathed the air of this world. Back then, we were certain that we'd stay true to our commitment no matter what challenges we would ultimately face, and we were right about that - despite our fresh set of financially-challenged circumstances, being away from Eric still was not an option.

So, as Gary hit the ground running in an intense attempt to find a new job, it was clear that *my* job search would never get off the ground. There were plenty of employment options available out there with plenty of money to be made, but even in this most desperate of times, no amount of money was worth letting somebody else raise Eric. Who knows, maybe Eric wouldn't have minded. Maybe he was getting tired of spending all of his days and nights with me, but, if that was the case, I figured I could always apologize to him later. I, personally, couldn't imagine spending my days away from him. Eric had become my career and I loved going to work each day! I couldn't … I wouldn't … give that up.

I thank God every day for allowing me to choose to be with Eric while he grew and learned. My dual role of full-time mom/businessperson may not have been the least stressful choice, but it was certainly very rewarding. It proved to me that anything is possible. It was difficult at times, but Eric and I made it work. I will always be thankful to my dad for giving me the opportunity to work while taking care of Eric. Eric benefited and I benefited. It allowed our family to stay in our current home, planting our roots in a place where we could live for a very long time. Again, had my dual-role arrangement not been an option, we would have moved into a more affordable situation so that I could stay at home with Eric full-time. The only thing that mattered to me was to be an integral part of Eric's childhood and it was up to me to make the choices allowing me to reach that goal. Yes, I was stressed out sometimes. Yes, sometimes I sat and cried, thinking that I wasn't meeting anyone's needs, not even my own. That was to be expected though. Who doesn't get overwhelmed by intense multitasking and lots of huge changes happening all at once?! Through it all, I have continued to believe that, when it comes to raising children, there is no good substitute for Mommy.

Why have I always felt this way? What causes different women to have very different opinions regarding the priority order of motherhood? Obviously, situations and experiences throughout our lives slowly mold us into the adults that we become. And aside from "just knowing" that being a stay-at-home mom was the right role for me, I can't really put my finger on any one single experience that swayed me in that direction. Part of my reasoning could have been based on the assumption that parenting *must* become my full-time job if I expect to do it well. Also, as I pointed out earlier, I feel certain that my own mother played a role in influencing my beliefs, as she stayed at home with me and my brother while we were growing up. I have great memories of our time together, and there was never any need to question the order of her priorities. Not only did she seem content in her role as "Mommy," but she also seemed to enjoy it quite a bit. Of course, given that era, there weren't many socially acceptable options other than staying at home with the kids full-time. However, even with the alternatives acceptable today, I'm certain that my mother still would have chosen her stay-at-home mom role. If I were a child today, it would have meant a lot to me had my mom made the choice to be with me. Knowing her potential capabilities apart from raising me, my thoughts probably would've gone something like this: "Mom is smart. She could be a corporate big-wig somewhere and bring home a bigger paycheck than Dad, if she wanted to. But she wants to stay with me. Wow. I must be important. She must really like me to want to be with me all day." My point is that I know that I would've sensed the feelings behind her decision, even if I was too young to piece it into those words.

It's true that most kids today are living in a much different world than I lived in when I was a kid. I guess that's another function of my old friend *time*. Thanks to time, there's change. And as long as time never stops, neither will change. So I suppose it's not surprising that, over the years, change has affected our roles and lifestyles. In its own right, that isn't such a bad thing. The potential problem lies in the fact that, along with the changes in roles, the natural order of priorities has also changed for many. I think that's a bad change.

Our modern society seems to make it almost acceptable that people "try" parenting without really committing to it. That may sound ridiculous, but I've met both men and women who actually treat parenting as though it's something that they can quit if they don't like doing it. Before I got pregnant, I had no clue whether I'd like being a parent. Obviously I thought that I would, or else I would not have gotten pregnant in the first place. Still, I realized there was no turning back once the pregnancy test read positive and that, even if I ended up hating being a mom, I'd have no choice but to live with it, with a positive attitude, for the rest of my life.

Thankfully, I quickly figured out that I like being a parent. Eric is not a hobby. He's not a last ditch alternative to fill up extra time that *may* be available after the adequate completion of work or chores or adult conversation. In fact, the reverse is true. When I chose to give birth I committed to parenting and had no doubts about the acceptable priority order of my son and the rest of my wants and needs. I knew, from that point on, that my son would come first. I'm thankful that I had no doubts about this.

It must be tough for those women who are uncertain about the order of their priorities. I can't imagine trying to determine what's best for Eric and me without "just knowing." How would I figure it out? Maybe I'd look to the outside for help. The latest research results on parenting could be a good place to start. Or perhaps I would consider the possible difficulties of my new maternal role - potential feelings of boredom or need for adult dialogue. Maybe the impending tedium of being confined to my house with only mono-syllabic words to be exchanged would affect my decision as to where to place Eric on my list of priorities.

I'm happy to say that the "tedium" and "boredom" and "need for adult dialogue" to which I refer are foreign to me. You see, I have always communicated with beings that, well, couldn't communicate back. Yes, it was just Eric's luck that he was being raised by parents who talked *to* their dog, and talked *for* their dog! It is a well-known fact amongst our friends and relatives that Sigmund, our little nine-pound toy poodle, has the benefit of being able to communicate verbally and have his opinions and thoughts considered by Gary and me. I am aware that this sounds strange, but it has certainly made for a more interesting human/dog relationship over the years.

Unfortunately, I would venture to guess that many women don't relish the prospect of a one-way conversation with their dog, let alone with their infant. Even if they do, why resort to that? After all, nowadays there are so many other socially-accepted options available to help lessen the severity of lifestyle changes for overwhelmed new moms. Is there anything wrong with taking advantage of some of these options? Probably not, if done in moderation. However, I do believe that pre-pregnancy, rather than post-birth, is a better time to consider, and emotionally adjust to, all of the lifestyle changes and perceived inconveniences caused by motherhood.

Once I became pregnant with Eric, *my* needs took a backseat. I didn't need research results or the opinions of experts to tell me the "right" thing to do regarding my son. I conceived him and ultimately gave birth to him, so it is my responsibility to raise him. Nothing short of a lack of the bare necessities would have changed my mind, despite being a member of our "want-it-all, have-it-all" society. I felt that there was way too much at stake to consider the fashionable alternatives.

I've met quite a few moms who are torn between their kids and their career. This isn't surprising given that women prepare for a successful career the same way men do these days. College, technical training, movement up the corporate ladder – it's the same track taken by our male counterparts and difficult to throw away if and when we get the childbearing "pang." As I see it though, it's a misconception that we are throwing away anything. I have various identities (and, some may argue, personalities) that make me who I am. I am daughter. I am wife. I am business person. And now, I am mommy. Each role has contributed to the next, and has not been wasted or thrown away. I can pull from my experiences any time that the need arises, and, at any time, I can decide to re-prioritize my roles. For instance, I haven't lost Sue, the business person. She is merely behind the scenes right now. If and when I need to move her back to center stage, she will be there.

In addition to the fear of wasting all of that career training and preparation, there are certainly many other tempting reasons to resume a career after kids are born. For one, continuing with a full-time career may set the family up very well financially. The kids won't want for anything material, which certainly seems like a nice perk.

If I were to consider returning to work based on financial wants instead of needs, I would first ask Eric if that is what he would prefer. If he was too young to understand the question, then *that* would be the answer to my question – he certainly needs his mommy more than "things."

Maybe I'm being naïve by thinking that not very many children, if any at all, would actually want their mom to leave them to go to work each day if they had a choice in the matter. The reality is, however, that kids aren't given a choice. Instead, they are at the mercy of their parents' choices. If mommy really wants to go back to work, her children can't stop her. On the other hand, there are plenty of moms out there who must work full-time just to make ends meet. That's a tough situation and not one based on want, but rather, need. Can kids tell the difference? I believe they can.

Does Eric ever think about the choices that Gary and I make? Does he understand why we do the things we do? I wonder if it fazes him one way or the other, or if he considers any choice that we make just "the way it is." Could he sense if I wanted to be apart from him? Could he sense if it tears me up inside to be apart from him?

I truly believe that I would've known the difference between my mother *having* to work to help support our family and my mother *choosing* to work based on her own wants. I'm sure I would have seen sadness in her eyes and felt it in her touch, had necessity forced her to be away from me when she really didn't want to be. Not only that, but it would've taken only a few days without adequate food or clothing before *I* would have suggested that mom should get a job! The bare necessities are the bare necessities, after all. But if my mother's decision to work outside the house was strictly a choice between me and a fancy Mercedes or if she worked away from home so that she and dad could afford an annual spa vacation ... well ... that would've been a different matter altogether. Would there have been sorrow in her eyes? How would that have affected me? How would it have affected my self worth? I can only guess. All I know for sure is that children are young, but they are not stupid.

As I said before, if I didn't "just know" the right choice for Eric and me, I may have depended upon the so-called experts to educate me regarding the best route to take. There is a ton of research out there supporting the choices of both stay-at-home and working moms, and I was actually able to find one consistent thread of information between the two opinions: young children benefit when they are in the constant company of an individual whom they can trust and with whom they can build a relationship. And, to make things a bit easier, this trusted person does not have to be related to the child for the child to benefit positively. Wow! That means I could have put Eric in daycare because there would have been plenty of people there with whom he could build relationships! I do have one question: *who are all of those people?*

The bottom line for me is that I want, unconditionally, to be the person to raise Eric. I knew all along that motherhood would cause my life to change drastically. I knew all along that, at least early in motherhood, I probably wouldn't have much adult interaction. I knew that sometimes it would probably be pretty inconvenient to be a mom. I didn't choose to be a stay-at-home mom because of theories or expert opinions or research results. I chose this path because it was the only way that I could guarantee that Eric was receiving the best care based on our standards. I chose this path because, for me, the whole point of having a son was to spend time with him and get to know him inside and out and build a solid relationship with him. Once we made that <u>pre-birth</u> commitment, we did everything in our power to create the situation that allowed us to follow through with our commitment - budgeting, downsizing, whatever.

I'm sure I'd appreciate that there are other socially-accepted options out there if my feelings or financial situation were different. Clearly, there are many women who are completely dependent on those options for mere financial or personal survival. As for the other moms out there who are dependent on those options purely based on desire rather than need, I wonder what motivated them to have children in the first place. Perhaps those women should spend an afternoon or two in the sandbox.

~ 6 ~

Happy Sounds

If a mother respects both herself and her child from his very first day onward, she will never need to teach him respect for others.

- ALICE MILLER

Speaking of the sandbox, once again I was in ours, this time taking on the highly respected role of assistant castle-builder, subordinate to Eric. I'd been fighting off, with all my might, the urge to continue philosophizing, as this setting seemed to provide a breeding ground for introspection. For a second I feared that all of the thoughts swirling through my brain would actually cause a water spout in the little moat surrounding our very impressive sandcastle! It was definitely time to return home to the present, but not without the valuable gifts contributed by the events of the recent past. I felt excitement, beyond words, with my life as a genuine stay-at-home mom, money or no money.

As I helped Eric put the finishing touches on our castle, I couldn't help but feel a sense of relief that I could focus completely on my son, without the distractions of work to which I had become so accustomed. It was the first time that I acknowledged how much energy it had truly taken to be in the moment with Eric while dealing with the issues of the business. Hopefully I had given him what he needed during that complex time. There was no going back, after all.

Just then, the phone rang. I was just beginning to figure out that I must lose the habit of carrying the phone with me wherever I go like I used to do when I was employed. At least I could no longer look forward to an endless parade of angry suppliers. Now, a ringing telephone pretty much guaranteed that either Gary or my mother was on the other end of the line. I answered timidly and realized that this time it was Gary, on his way back from an apparently successful interview. Unfortunately, one successful interview merely meant that there would be another interview, and so on, and so on. We quickly realized that places of business did not seem to have the same sense of urgency concerning the hiring process as we did. Still, relatively speaking, Gary's call could be considered good news.

After a short conversation, I placed the phone safely outside the perimeter of the sandbox and glanced down at our castle - or should I say the pile of sand that *was* our castle. Obviously, while I was pre-occupied with the phone call, our once-elaborate structure had been stomped on a multitude of times by the "Eric Monster." What a perfect illustration of the momentous damage that can be caused by losing track of the here-and-now even for just a few moments! Why do little kids like destruction just as much as, if not more than, construction? At least in Eric's case, there seemed to be just as much love and joy involved in dismantling a structure as there was in building it. Welcome to the world of little boys!

I decided that the time had come for me to determine how I'd protect our castle from future stompings. In order to do that successfully, I'd first need to control my hidden urge to excuse myself to finish my household chores. Admittedly, since becoming officially unemployed, I'd been experiencing slight twinges of guilt here and there for sitting and playing instead of doing something "productive." What a perfect illustration of the fact that "being there" for Eric was still a conscious decision to be made, stay-at-home mom or not. You see, staying at home presented me with plenty of diversions, aside from my son, that could potentially take me away from the very reason I chose to be there in the first place.

Then it dawned on me - deciding to live <u>in the moment</u> is one of the most essential choices that must be made in order to completely "be there" for Eric. My point is that, even though I'm at home with Eric, if I'm spending most of my time cleaning and doing whatever other chores need to be done (including philosophizing), then I may as well be at an office somewhere, because I'm certainly not with Eric in spirit. I think this matters.

So, in response to my own thoughts, I took a quick trip back to now and began to construct large walls around the mound of sand that was our castle. This surely would protect what was left of our structure. Or would it? Suddenly the Eric Monster appeared from the distance, intent upon destroying the newly built walls. The only thing that could stop him …. was …. was…. the hose! Mommy's quick thinking helped her win this round. The truth of the matter is that it was actually a win-win situation. Eric enjoyed getting sprayed *and* the walls of the castle were spared, at least for the time being. And me? Well, I loved listening to the happy sounds. Giggling is my favorite happy sound, and on that day I was getting my fair share of it from my water-logged little boy! I knew that the battle wouldn't end there, though. I was pretty sure we'd end up going another round or two before a winner was officially declared. The cool thing was that, by the looks of it, this just might be a memory that would stick.

Happy sounds: for as much as *I* enjoy them and am positively affected by them, I know that Eric is too. It's obvious by his expression that he loves to see me having fun, especially when we're having fun together. Obviously I would be doing Eric a great disservice if I was miserable in his presence day in and day out. I know that I can't have a bad attitude and still have quality time with my son. The two just don't mix. Actually, I read about a study that confirmed that parents who are oppressive, angry and unnurturing with their children have a negative effect on them, even if they spend twenty-four hours a day, seven days a week with them! I suppose it's always helpful to do a study that supports what common sense tells most of us.

Common sense or not, I must admit that reading about this research brought to mind moms I know who stay at home with their kids all day, but obviously are not happy about their arrangement. Even if these women pretend to be happy, can their kids tell that they would rather be somewhere else? I'm beginning to think that I have found my strong suit: presenting a lot of hypothetical questions to which I don't have the answers! Fortunately (or unfortunately), I do have opinions based on my own observations.

One thing I know for sure is that, despite his young age, Eric can see right through me. If I pretend to be happy when I'm actually sad, he knows it. Just when I think I've fooled him, "Mommy, what's wrong?" pops out of his mouth as evidence that I won't be winning any Academy Awards any time soon! I know - it could just be that I'm a bad actor, but I think kids rely more on instincts than adults do so they usually know how we're really feeling. They pay instinctive attention to obscure signals within body language and tone of voice that we adults tend to tune out. So, in my opinion, kids, no matter what their age, do know whether or not mom would rather be somewhere else.

Now the next rhetorical question: If I'm right about kids knowing our true feelings, what are the ramifications of kids knowing our true feelings? I mean, is it a good thing to be a stay-at-home mom if you really don't want to be? I believe the answer is "no." So then, if I'm right about that, what are the alternatives? Could Mom try to work out her feelings with a counselor? Absolutely. I don't think it's ever impossible to come to terms with a major life change, especially if we acknowledge when we need help doing so. After all, most life changes involve some form of loss, whether it's real or perceived. Motherhood is no different, since a new mom may perceive that she has lost her old self. A counselor may help her with the redefinition process or merely assist her with the development of a new perspective. The bottom line is that the feeling that "mommy doesn't like being with me" cannot possibly do anything good for a child's emotional health.

Although I have strong opinions, I do believe that everyone has a right to choose their own path. The fact is, whether you stay at home with your kids or are otherwise employed, being a good mom takes a lot of work and ongoing mental adjustments. For instance, once I came to the realization that staying home with Eric doesn't automatically make me a "good mom," I had to work hard to change my old perspective that regarded playtime as non-productive time. I had to start looking at it from the longer-term point-of-view. Although it may not seem like I'm getting anything important done at the time, the truth is that my quality time with

Eric will pay off more than any cleaning or household administrative task that I could choose to complete instead. I am building a human being. I am teaching a human being. If I choose to ignore that very important responsibility that became mine when Eric entered this world, I will be doing him, and the world, a great disservice. Not only that, but I have fun when I'm spending time with my son!

Without a doubt, quality time and positive perceptions are extremely important pieces of the parenting puzzle, and therefore, in my opinion, deserve a big chunk of print. However, an important question is "can quality make up for a lack of quantity?"

I'll explain why I *don't* think it can. Eric needs a lot of my time. He depends on me to be there for him whenever he needs me. Frighteningly, I read somewhere that parents today average only five and a half minutes of meaningful conversation with their children daily. Hmm, let me think. What could I possibly learn about Eric by spending such a small amount of time with him each day? Sometimes it takes him that long just to get one sentence out of his mouth! More often than not, little bits and pieces of important information about who this young person is pop up at different times throughout the day and night; things that he may not remember right away but that he wants to tell me, or questions that he may have specific to some activity that we are doing together at the time.

Look at it in a different way – if you went out to eat at the nicest restaurant in town and ordered the most expensive steak on the menu and ten minutes later the waiter returned with a plate containing a one-inch cube of steak, what would you do? Now, keep in mind that this is the finest piece of steak you can buy. It will be the best you've ever tasted. Does quantity really matter? I'll venture to guess that this miniscule piece of steak wouldn't satisfy you, and I KNOW it wouldn't satisfy me. I'd definitely be hungry for more. Would Eric really feel satisfied with just a tiny little chunk of my time? No. Also, when it comes to spending time with Eric, a combination of quality and quantity will help him feel like an insider within the family unit – give him a sort of interconnectedness. Instead of having a "his world" and a "my world," we have an "our world" which encompasses all of us – Gary, me, and Eric.

The point of making sure Eric knows that he matters to me more than anything else – engaging in conversation and activities with him, listening to his point of view and showing him the respect that I would show a peer – is, in my opinion, a very important aspect of "being there." Not only that, but I believe that interconnectedness means never feeling that the family bond has broken, no matter what problems or issues the parents or children are facing.

This brings me to another curious question. Why do some kids from broken or troubled families grow up to be happy, well-adjusted adults, while others from similar situations grow into adults who act out or have constant problems with relationships, substance abuse or a variety of other issues? Why don't these situations affect all children in the same way? Could "interconnectedness" with the family unit (or lack thereof) have anything to do with the outcome of these unfortunate scenarios? After all, a child pushed to the outside of his family unit during trying times is basically an isolated child, as he loses his most powerful, instinctive form of stability. And an isolated child is a child who must fend for himself emotionally, and maybe even physically. I believe that anytime a young child is forced to grow up prematurely, problems will tend to surface down the road.

I know that, whether or not it makes any sense, or whether or not it will actually play a role in Eric's ultimate happiness, it feels right to our family to include Eric in our world, complete with joy and pain, happiness and grief. I believe we're stronger as a team and, quite frankly, I couldn't imagine living any other way.

Speaking of "team," the third member of ours was apparently home. The sudden clanking sound of the garage door opening caused my thoughts to come to a screeching halt, sparing the reader from more of an ongoing slew of rhetorical questions. I was just finishing preparing Eric's favorite dinner of macaroni and cheese, when Gary entered with a smile, obviously feeling pretty good about his latest job opportunity.

After a quick greeting and short summary of his day, Gary hurried upstairs to change out of his coat and tie while I got Eric situated at the dinner table. That is when I found myself beginning to slip into deep thought once more.

I became engrossed in Eric's fine demonstration of manual dexterity as he ate his macaroni and cheese with his fingers. As I stared at him, I still couldn't believe how fast he was growing. Oddly, the kitchen table was where I found his growth most noticeable - it seemed like I could see more and more of his face over the table top with each meal! Oh well. This was just more subtle evidence of the incredible speed of time.

~ 7 ~

With Great Power Comes Great Responsibility

No influence is so powerful as that of the mother.
- SARAH JOSEPHA HALE

As time passed, so too did the childhood period void of good guys and bad guys. Suddenly Eric, who just a short while ago was thrilled by the noise of a rattle or the soft, cuddliness of his Elmo doll, was now consumed by the world of superheroes and arch enemies. I don't suppose there's anything wrong with that – I think it's a "guy thing," but the age of toy innocence had definitely come to an end.

Spiderman was the popular superhero of the time. Aggressively marketed as an action figure *and* a video game to promote "Spiderman: the Movie," it was no wonder why he was the superhero of choice for Eric. He begged to see the movie, so Gary and I decided to watch it first to determine if it was age-appropriate for Eric, which, in our opinion, it was not. However, since Eric was really only interested in seeing Spidey swing by his web from skyscraper to skyscraper, we allowed him to watch those scenes, carefully skipping over any violent parts with remote in hand.

Aside from providing Eric with quite a bit of entertainment, "Spiderman: The Movie" also made quite an impression on *me*, all because of the following quote from the "Uncle Ben" character to Peter Parker, a.k.a. Spiderman: "With great power, comes great responsibility." Fictional character or not, I think Uncle Ben hit the nail on the head. Spiderman has superhuman powers that must be well thought out prior to being utilized, or else he will risk harming people rather than helping them. But Uncle Ben's statement doesn't just apply to Spiderman. Moms have incredible powers too, the most notable being the power of influence. And if we choose to use this power, we, too, must do so responsibly, or we could cause more damage than even Spiderman could imagine!

Influence is a concept that, in a sense, piggy-backs "being there." When Eric is with us, in our world, he is influenced by our choices, our moods, and our reactions. He may not want to be, but he can't help it. It just happens. Likewise, if Eric spent a great deal of his time in daycare or with other members of our family, he would be most influenced by those individuals.

I would be remiss if I failed to elaborate on the huge responsibility that goes along with the power of influence - a responsibility greater than any other. Essentially, those who hold this power are affecting the outcome of other people's lives. And since we all influence one another quite frequently throughout our lives, it would be well to take that into consideration when choosing how to behave, how to speak and, in general, how to live. In other words, we must consider the fact that we all are accidental role models to the people we encounter. We could make the excuse that human beings aren't perfect, so the reality is that overall, we will all be poor role models, so why worry about it? But we should worry about it, or at least take it into consideration when making choices. We need to do that for the sake of the world. We need to do that for the sake of another human being's potential. *I* need to do that for the sake of my son because, as I have said many times before, it was *my* choice to bring Eric into this world, not his, so I owe it to him to take my power of influence seriously, with his best interest in mind. This represents yet another reason for my decision to stay at home with Eric: because no other person on this earth is going to take their power of influence over my son more seriously than I do.

As Eric gets older and needs answers to the multitude of questions filling his mind, I expect that he will seek out an individual who he trusts and respects, probably one with whom he has a high comfort level, to help him answer those questions. It also seems logical that he will turn to the person or people with whom he spends a great deal of time. I am hoping that, since Gary and I spend a lot of time with Eric, he will turn to us for answers first. I also believe that his instincts will play a role in this choice. I believe that young children instinctively turn to their parents for guidance unless their parents cannot or do not contribute, at which point the kids will turn elsewhere, possibly to peers or teachers. Obviously this happens some of the time no matter how well-connected we are with our kids, but I believe that when kids turn to others as the rule rather than the exception, it is a sure-fire sign that family communication has broken down and problems could be on the horizon.

Not only is it my goal to fully utilize my power of influence toward Eric, but I also hope to never take this power for granted, nor knowingly abuse it. One of my favorite songs, "Circle of Steel" by Gordon Lightfoot, really drives this point home. It is a song about parental influence gone awry and it makes me cry every time I hear it. It relays the experience of a child watching his mother drink all day while his father is in prison – an extreme situation, but it's the point of it that matters. One of the lines is "…she tips the gin bottle back till it's gone, the child is strong." Clearly the family portrayed in the song was in a bad situation, plagued by bad decisions made by both the mom and the dad. Although their circumstances may have been extreme, not to mention fictional, these lyrics illustrate the point that young kids have no alternative but to endure the consequences of their parents' choices. Who held the power to influence this child? The mother, who was drunk and suffering in her own right, and the father, who obviously had quite serious troubles of his own.

It's so true that kids are strong. First and foremost, they can't choose their parents. Let's face it - some kids have been dealt a hand of cards that is pretty bad, right off the bat. Then, when you consider all of the changes they must go through - physical and emotional growth, going to school for the first time, mastering language, socialization, learning how friends hurt them sometimes - the list goes on and on. It's truly amazing. And then when you think about the fact that the people who are supposed to take complete care of them and protect them sometimes falter – albeit, at different severity levels – that has got to be devastating for a child.

It's so important for kids to know that they are loved by, and can depend on, their parents. That is why I am very careful in determining how to best use my power of influence with Eric, because, when all is said and done, the responsibility for his happiness or sadness, self-confidence or self-degradation, along with many other aspects of his life, will fall on Gary and me. We are the ones responsible for providing him with the necessary tools to build a happy and fulfilling life, and we will always take that self-imposed responsibility very seriously.

Is it possible that our kids actually want our influence? I believe so. Eric doesn't yet have the tools necessary to thrive in this world. If Gary and I don't take on the job of seeing that he gets them, Eric will have to manage without these tools, which will put him at quite a disadvantage. For instance, if he doesn't feel strong enough to be away from us once he's of school age, what will happen? If he doesn't have a clue as to how to interact with his own age group, what will happen? If he doesn't know the difference between right and wrong, what will happen? If he doesn't understand the meaning of respect, or responsibility – what will happen? One thing that will surely happen is that Eric will suffer. He will have adjustment issues. He will have disciplinary problems. He'll end up associating with other kids who have similar issues and his level of confidence will deteriorate. Don't get me wrong, I will never have complete control over Eric, nor do I want that. However I do want to take advantage of my position on the front line of influence so at least I have the first shot.

It appears to me that many of the social and behavioral issues of modern kids have the distinct markings of emotional suffering. That makes sense if the people to whom these children look for communication, care, and time, are not there for them. As I pointed out in the last chapter, I read that five and a half minutes of meaningful conversation per day is the norm between kids and their parents. I don't think it's humanly possible to give a child what he needs in that amount of time. Most of us try our very best to be good parents, so how can that number possibly be so low? Perhaps the belief that it's most important to give our children more *stuff* than we had has been passed down through the generations. More clothes. Better clothes. More toys. Bigger toys. Perhaps some of us feel that, if we provide our kids with an overabundance of material goods, they will be happy, know that they are loved and live better lives. And let's face it, based on the pace of our lives, sometimes providing materially is the easiest route to take. We must stop and think for a moment though. Are our children really better off with more things? Or, would they rather have mom actively involved in their life for more than five minutes per day? If a child is having problems with aggression or acting out at school, could it be that he simply needs mom's influence to help him be who he was meant to be? Yes. I believe that "being there" for our children, not "stuff," will provide them with the initial, most important building blocks for a happy future.

The other day I was reading a book about birds to Eric. It was really interesting because it explained how birds develop and grow from the time that they hatch through adulthood. It illustrated the manner in which the mommy bird takes care of her young chicks until they are ready to fly. At that point it struck me that all the creatures of nature do that very same thing! Each species stays with its mother or father for a certain amount of time before it leaves the nest, den, or other secure setting. In the wild this is an instinctive situation, so there are no options other than that, otherwise the young will not survive. I mean, could you imagine if every day at dawn just after feeding time a mother bluebird grabbed her baby bluebird by the neck and flew her over to another nest where there were bluebirds, blue jays, crows, doves and cardinals all chirping away and all having very different needs? Of course there would be a very competent female bird there to care for the young chicks while the mother bluebird flew away to spend the day with other birds her own age. All I can say is, let's just hope that the wildlife population continues to rely only on instinct!

The human world isn't all that dissimilar from the bird world in the sense that human young need somebody to tend to them until they are ready to "spread their wings" and survive - or, to take it one step further, to "thrive" on their own. Yes, *thrive*. Houghton-Mifflin has defined the word "thrive" as "to make steady progress; prosper" or "to grow vigorously; flourish." I believe that this word represents one of the major differences between wild animals - including birds - and human beings. Wild animals deal frequently with real issues of *physical* thriving and survival whereas humans deal more frequently with the issues of *emotional* thriving and survival. So, as long as we humans are surviving *physically*, we seem to be extremely tolerant of any <u>inability</u> to thrive emotionally and therefore will not necessarily see any reason to change our way of living.

On the flip side, if our kids in daycare were dying left and right, then we'd surely notice and likely make changes. However, I believe that our inability to thrive emotionally *is* an inability to fully live because we are in a constant emotional struggle. I suppose the bottom line is: if physical survival is what we are shooting for, then it hardly matters who takes care of our young and for how long, as long as the young are provided with adequate food, drink and shelter. On the other hand, if we want our children to thrive, then it may take more than the influence of a paid caregiver to make that happen. You may be thinking "Proof! Give me proof!" Well, once you have absolute, rock-solid proof, it will be too late. <u>Faith</u> is what is needed - <u>faith</u> in your reason for becoming a mom in the first place how ever many years ago; <u>faith</u> that the world will indeed be a better place because of your commitment to your kids now and in the future.

Not to obsess over the bird book, but, just like "Spiderman: The Movie," it really got me thinking. Many of the questions that popped into my head after reading that book have been rhetorical (as usual). There are still some questions, however, that are not rhetorical in the least and probably can be answered quite easily. One such question is: "Are *my* needs being met as a stay-at-home mom?" I relied on my instincts to determine that I would stay home with Eric. I "just knew" that this was the right thing for me to do. Does that, in itself, mean that my needs are being met? For me, the answer is yes. I find my role as stay-at-home mom both enjoyable and fulfilling so I can state, with no doubt, that my needs are being met - <u>at least the needs that matter the most to me right now</u>. I can't be in the minority with this answer, can I?

If I am in the minority, the difference may be that I have chosen to define my needs based on my expectations, rather than to define my expectations based on my needs. For example, while Eric is still young, I don't expect to have an abundance of one-on-one time with other adults, so I have chosen to place that need on the back burner. This is similar to the manner by which I regard my various "identities." No one identity ever really goes away, it just may not be on center stage at a given point in time. When the time is appropriate for me and my family, I will bring specific needs and/or identities back into focus.

As I mentioned earlier, over the course of the last few years I've heard various stay-at-home moms complain about their roles. Some of these moms were just plain bored without the adult interaction to which they had previously been accustomed. Others had been engrossed in their careers before they had kids and now felt as though they had lost a very important part of themselves and longed to have it back. This brings me to the one word that I believe to be the key to dealing with these feelings: *patience*.

Sometimes we adults are no more patient than young children. Just as an impatient young child may ask "Are we there yet?" over and over again until their desired destination is in plain sight, an impatient adult tends to *complain* over and over again until his or her desired destination is in plain sight! Don't allow your current impatience or displeasure with motherhood to become a negative focus of your conversation, especially in front of your kids. Please consider how you would have felt had your mother openly voiced displeasure about being your mom. Realize that the speed of time is such that you'll get any perceived "missing" parts of yourself back faster than you could ever imagine.

That being said, by the time we grow into adulthood we hopefully realize (or resort to therapy to find out) that how our parents treated us or how they felt about their parental roles *should not* be the determining factor in our own self-respect or perceived value. I place the emphasis on *should not* because this is a very difficult concept to swallow as a mature adult, let alone as a small child. A small child is reacting on instinct alone - his instincts are telling him that there's a person around, perhaps with the name of "Mommy," who he can fully trust and who will most lovingly fill each of his needs. My gut tells me that if a young child concludes that this instinct is wrong, he'll begin to question all of his instincts.

I'm certainly not suggesting that a stay-at-home mom has to be a constant Carol Brady, always smiling and happy while spending ninety-nine percent of her waking hours playing with, and entertaining, her kids. Still, there is a big difference between being down or frustrated once in a while and being generally unhappy about your maternal situation, stay-at-home or not. The kids can tell. They need you to be there for them, to make them your first priority, and then they will feel safe and have the ability to follow their instincts without question. These young people look to their mothers for all that they are and all that they need. In their eyes, mothers speak only truth. Mothers know all.

If you are a stay-at-home mother who is bored with your role, I want to remind you that, when you look at your son or daughter, you are actually looking at a potential masterpiece. It is up to you to provide the frame for their unique work of art. Spend your spare time giving them plenty of love, support and influence so that they are able to paint their own picture to their fullest potential. If you use your time for this purpose beginning right now, you'll ultimately have an abundance of the proof that you originally wanted - proof that, through your commitment to your children, you are making the world a better place.

The other day, just for fun, I was imagining motherhood from a corporate perspective. Interestingly, the sort of make-believe scenario that I created seemed to me to do a good job of illustrating the level of importance of the role of "mommy." I am hoping that this perspective will prove interesting especially for those moms who feel that they have lost a part of themselves while staying at home to raise their kids. On the other hand, if it seems, well ... too goofy, please just bear with me!

First, imagine that you are, indeed, a professional and you have just been hired by a very successful corporation called "Mommy, Inc." Your boss has given you a huge, incredibly important assignment to work on all day long every day. He has given you a list of short-term and long-term goals and deadlines for the project. Your boss has advised you to begin work on your short-term goals first, because, if you are successful in reaching those goals, you will likely be successful reaching your long-term goals too. And, by the way, if you complete this assignment successfully, the results are guaranteed to positively change the world. However, while your project will make the world a *better* place if completed successfully, on the flip side, miscommunication or lack of attention to the project will have far-reaching negative implications.

Is there any actual corporate project out there that is this critically important? I'm sure that there is. Whoever is responsible for such a project is probably a very highly-paid, high-profile corporate executive. My question is, "What is the difference between raising children and working to complete a high-level corporate project?" After all, both require an incredible amount of time, effort and dedication to have any hope of success. Actually, as I see it, the only true differences between the two are money and hours. Obviously, my job of stay-at-home mom to Eric does not provide me with a formal paycheck, nor does it provide me with any time off. In fact, I am on call twenty-four hours a day, seven days a week. Hmm. I wonder what the dollar value actually is for each of my "mommy" responsibilities. What would my salary level likely be? It's definitely a curious thought, especially because I am quite certain that the responsibilities associated with being a mother hold an even higher level of importance then those of a top corporate job. So, next time you're feeling that you desperately want that corporate-mogul piece of you back, look at motherhood as a top-level executive position and climb *that* corporate ladder until your heart is content!

Honestly, I hadn't meant to focus so much on the naysayer mommies out there, because the truth is it's not all bad. There are plenty of moms, both stay-at-home and not, who are very aware of, and celebrate the importance of, their "mommy" role. In fact, I know quite a few women who are great examples of moms who "get it." There is one woman in particular, however, whose outspoken desire to be at home with her son really stands out. Bear with me while I step away from the here and now to go back in time for a minute or two.

The woman to whom I refer is named Heidi and she happens to be the mother of Brody, Eric's best friend from preschool. Heidi is a single mom with a full-time career. Her career is a necessity and she is very outspoken about her sadness that she isn't able to be a full-time stay-at-home mom to her son. It is quite obvious that Brody is precious to her and that she cherishes every moment she spends with him.

One day, after dropping Eric off at preschool, I noticed that some of the moms, including Heidi, were standing around chatting. It turned out that the talk amongst them was all about kindergarten. I willingly joined the conversation, eager to tell of my angst over Eric's ultimate and quickly approaching growth past the preschool stage. Heidi, specifically, shared my concern and went on to admit that, as of late, she hadn't been able to stop crying at night because of her obsession with Brody's next big step into Kindergarten the following year. She felt concerned but hopeful that she's not only given him what he needs to survive "out there" but also has instilled in him the values and morals that will keep him strong as he becomes even more independent. As usual, I could completely relate to how Heidi was feeling.

We've been given a basically uninterrupted time through toddlerhood to do what we can – to influence our children to the best of our ability. But when have we done enough? Have we fully taken advantage of this short amount of time to fill them with what they will need to thrive as they grow? It's not that we can't continue to teach them or influence them after they reach school-age, but it may become more difficult to make our influence count admidst peers, teachers and the outside world in general. Nevertheless, Heidi is one woman who clearly considers her power of influence to be an incredibly important element of being a mommy. She is very smart.

Although influence is a somewhat automatic result of "being there," there are a few communication- and relationship-oriented details that I believe help make Eric just a little more open to my influence. The first is mutual respect. Honestly, will I really be able to influence somebody who doesn't respect me? I know that I tend to listen to those individuals for whom I have the most respect. Little things like maintaining eye contact with Eric and physically getting down to his level while we are talking or while I am listening to him are a couple of things that I try to do to show him respect. After all, when I'm in a conversation with a friend, I try to maintain eye contact so that person knows I'm interested in what she's saying, so why shouldn't I do it with my own son? The bottom line is that maintaining eye contact with Eric shows him that I'm paying attention - that what he has to say is important. He deserves that.

Taking each one of Eric's questions seriously is also essential in influencing him. "Because" is not a good answer. Again, I wouldn't answer a friend's question with "because." If I did, I don't think my friend would be too thrilled about it. So, since I don't answer friends' questions that way, why would I answer Eric in that manner? I know that Eric depends on Gary and me for answers to his questions. They may not seem like important questions to us at the time, but to Eric they are extremely important. Using "because" as an answer to those questions conveys that we are not taking him seriously, and that's not "being there" and it's certainly not helping to influence him. I look at my answers to Eric as small, quick life lessons. Serious answers to his questions help him to understand these lessons the first time he asks, so he doesn't have to repeat questions over and over. It's easy to get annoyed by a young child who continues to ask the same question again and again, but the case may actually be that the parent hasn't answered the child the first time! Whose fault is that?

On the flip side of answering questions is, of course, asking questions. This was another one of my accidental discoveries. I used to ask Eric questions from birth on, due to my own need to have a conversation with him. Silly as it may sound, at first I asked *and* answered the questions, attempting to do so in a manner that I thought would closely parallel what his answers would eventually be. The day came suddenly when I no longer needed to play his part in Mommy-Eric discussions, however. Suddenly he began to respond. Of course his answers were in broken English initially, but I understood, as moms tend to do, even when other people didn't. As time went on, Eric began to expect me to ask questions. In fact, to this day he is fully prepared to sit down and have the "Mommy and Eric Talk" over snacks and milk after visits with friends or with grandparents, and especially after school. Of course I'm very interested in what he's doing and how he's feeling when we're apart, but I have also set the stage for him to expect that I'm always going to ask questions. As he gets older, he may very well become annoyed by my questions, but one thing's for sure: there will never be a doubt in his mind that I am interested in what's going on in his life.

Gary and I always want Eric to feel comfortable telling us anything, no matter how bad he thinks it is; essentially, be a sort of safety zone for him. Believe it or not, despite Eric's young age, we've already had several opportunities to test this concept. You see, without fail, each new school year has brought with it new questions regarding the appropriateness, or lack thereof, of certain words. It's been quite obvious that Eric has absolutely no problem communicating whatever "bad" word happens to be in question at the time. Although having to deal with this type of issue at such a young age could be considered sad rather than funny, it is nevertheless humorous to witness the serious concern on our little guy's face as we try to explain whether or not the word in question is appropriate to say. Regardless, our main goal will continue to be never to go off on a tirade, as long as Eric is honest with us. We've been successful so far, but I'm sure it won't get any easier.

If Gary and I are going to attempt to influence Eric, it only makes sense for us to do so in a positive manner. In other words, as I touched on earlier, we must be good role models to our son. What, exactly, defines a good role model? That's the tough part. The definition of a good role model is often no more than a matter of personal opinion. For instance, although I could never imagine such a thing (sarcasm), some of the actions or characteristics that Gary and I consider acceptable for our family may not be acceptable to the next family. So, although we can teach Eric what we consider to be good behavior, what ultimately will matter the most is that he develops *strength of character* – a certainty about his own belief system that will allow him to adapt to whatever life throws at him. When will that happen? Actually, it's <u>always</u> happening.

~ 8 ~

Building Character

Men are what their mothers made them.

- RALPH WALDO EMERSON

Character: an extremely subjective, though much sought-after, result of influence. Building character: a phrase that I find misleading, despite its prominence as the title of this chapter! Why do I consider it misleading? Well, it gives the impression that we *build* our own character, when I don't think it happens quite that way. Instead, life builds character for us from birth until death through all of the trials and tribulations we must endure, some of which are under our control, while others are not.

Ideally, I'd love to protect Eric from all potentially painful experiences that life may throw at him – provide him with a nice, safe cocoon in which to grow and develop. Unfortunately, that's not possible, and even if it were, it probably wouldn't end up being such a great idea anyway. So instead, I must get a jump start on helping him prepare for the variety of situations that may lie ahead. To do this successfully, I must focus on my power of influence early in order to help him learn to control the only thing that he *can* control in response to life's twists and turns: his reaction. (Oh, and by the way - he doesn't need to know that Mommy hasn't yet mastered the very skill that she is trying to teach him!)

Although I hate to admit it, I'm not the first person to buy into the idea that character development is a life-long process. A very long time ago, Eleanor Roosevelt was quoted in saying that "character building begins in our infancy and continues until death." But what exactly is "character" anyway? Merriam-Webster defines *character* as "one of the attributes or features that make up and distinguish an individual." Another definition in that same dictionary is "moral excellence and firmness." I believe attributes like honesty, kindness, dependability, patience and respect represent the traits of a person of good character, whereas violence, dishonesty, impatience, greed and hatred are representative of someone with questionable character. To me, quite simply, character is about trying to do the right thing.

For Eric's sake, Gary and I don't feel comfortable waiting for his peers, teachers, or anyone else to venture into the uncharted territory of character development with him. This too must begin with us. But how? Well, I figure that, assuming that we do indeed learn from our experiences, the earlier that Eric is exposed to a variety of situations, the sooner he will begin to develop his own sense of character. Based on that assumption, perhaps our early conversations and interactions with Eric provided this additional unexpected benefit. I think so. Even something as simple as playing blocks with him helped with his character development, though. Gary and I just happened to jump ahead a few steps and let Eric in on a wide variety of social situations a little bit sooner than what may be typical. For instance, as soon as he was born we treated him as we would a peer by doing things like formally introducing him to people he had never met and addressing him politely with "please" and "thank you." I believe this provided Eric with communication-based character guidelines very early on even though he may not have completely understood what we were doing at the time. Only time will tell if those guidelines have truly become engrained in our little boy. His current behavior certainly leaves us hopeful.

I'll admit that it was pretty easy to focus on an infant's character development. For many reasons, the next stage, toddlerhood, proved to be a more challenging stage from a character-building standpoint. First and foremost, since Eric could now understand almost everything that came out of our mouths, Gary and I had to focus more than ever on kindness, respect and the elimination of bad-mouthing and negativity.

Negativity is one communication-oriented bad habit that manifests itself in all of us from time to time, and simply needs to be kicked for good! Unfortunately, little ears hear everything, especially bad words and cruelty. It never ceases to amaze me that I could be in a conversation that is ninety-nine percent positive and joyful and then have one complaint or criticism about somebody or something, and that is the one thing that Eric hears and happily repeats.

I know that my parents taught me that if I don't have anything nice to say I shouldn't say anything, but somewhere along the line it changed to "if I don't have anything nice to say, I can at least tell Gary," or something to that effect. My own negative talk about the way things are, whether that has to do with friends, family, responsibilities, or whatever else, will only lead Eric to do the same. It's called pessimism and there's really no point to it. Deep down I've always known this, but, despite trying my very best to avoid it, there are many times when I allow this attitude to manifest itself in words and actions that don't do anybody any good.

Gary and I try to focus on being positive so Eric will do the same. Is it any wonder why I consider this to be one of the toughest challenges of motherhood?! I know I can't possibly be perfect, but I can be more aware, which is a good first step. For instance, nowadays, instead of just babbling on, not realizing the implications of my words when I'm upset, frustrated or hormonal, I'll just take a break. Sitting down and watching a funny cartoon with Eric can do wonders to help me chill out. Getting out for a walk or run also works quite well (and is even better, from a health standpoint), as does yoga, which ranks right up there as a great stress-reliever when I'm angry or upset. Any one of these options definitely beats the alternative. This all gets back to the role-modeling component of being Mommy. In order to help Eric develop a good sense of character, we have to positively influence him. Being a positive influence to Eric is the same as being a positive role model. And this responsibility falls on Gary and me because Eric spends most of his time with us right now and because he looks to us for answers.

It's tough to be a role model. Or rather it's tough to be a *good* role model. Once again, "with great power comes great responsibility." On one hand, it is really cool that Eric wants to imitate our words and actions. On the other hand, this really puts pressure on us to do the right thing! We all will falter. After all, we're human and, as such, mere everyday stressors can sometimes swing our moods like a pendulum. Even that is important for Eric to realize, though – that, as humans, we all will make mistakes along the way. There! I've finally found my niche! I'm certain that I can teach Eric the old "humans make mistakes" lesson very easily! Seriously though, one thing I do know for sure is that my job as role model to Eric will never end so I may as well try to master the art of practicing what I preach.

That brings me to my least-enjoyable Mommy responsibility related to character-building: discipline. Obedience is the desired result of discipline. Obedience is not one of my favorite words because it brings to mind something that I've attempted to teach Sigmund, our dog! The truth is that Eric, like the rest of us, will most likely have to "obey" somebody, other than us, at some point in his life. That's why Gary and I are obligated to expose him to this chilling concept, for his own good and for the good of those around him. Good behavior and bad behavior and right and wrong must be defined and identified for Eric. Abiding by a well-preserved tradition, he, like most kids, tests limits. I feel strongly that this is actually his way of communicating that he wants to know the limits. Since Gary and I care about him so much and are most concerned for his well-being, I believe that we are the best ones to define those limits for him.

So what is discipline? Please excuse my excessive use of the dictionary, but I want to be as accurate as possible with my definitions. Merriam-Webster defines discipline as "training that corrects, molds, or perfects the mental faculties or moral character." Now this is just one of a few definitions, but it's my favorite. Discipline doesn't have to refer to "punishment" per se, although it very well may get to that level if the "training" isn't successful. It's evident that, in today's society, this so-called "training" needs to be stepped up a bit, especially because so much of the next level of discipline - punishment - has been rendered inappropriate or even criminal. So what can we moms do? We don't feel right about punishing our children, but they clearly need the limits defined and enforced. How does that happen?

For me, being in the presence of Eric, taking the time to model good behavior and define behavioral limits has been the only way to even attempt to eliminate the need for harsh punishment. But what happens when a child is not punished for bad behavior, but also has no idea what behavior is considered to be inappropriate behavior in the first place? My guess is that the child will continue to test limits until somebody reacts. Not only that, but the child will be forced to make his own judgment calls. At two years old? At three years old? Couldn't that potentially be a problem?

I am a firm believer that punishment can be nearly eliminated by paying attention to character early. Very early. Eric recognized the word "no" when he was very young because we used that word when he was very young. He may not have understood what we were saying at first, but it didn't take long for him to learn. I know of a mom who took an opposite tack on this subject, however. When her son was a toddler, the only way she could stop him from doing something that she didn't want him to do, like banging a toy on the nice living room table, was to take the toy from him and place it well out of his reach. Well, he'd eventually get that toy back or grab something else in his hand and resume his banging. Needless to say, this woman was growing quite frustrated until one weekend when her mother was babysitting her son. After the woman returned home and began to converse with her mom, her son began to bang on the table again. This time the grandmother addressed the boy with "no" in a stern voice. He immediately stopped banging and went on to play nicely. The woman then confessed to her mother that she didn't think her son understood the word "no." Her mother replied "Well, he does now." It's safe to say that kids won't understand words that aren't used. The earlier you say it, the earlier they'll pick it up.

Since I'm on the topic of discipline, I can't help but share two of my major pet peeves in this regard. The first one has to do with the differentiation between "being" and "doing." I can't tell you how many times I've overheard a mother call her child a "bad boy" or a "bad girl." This really bothers me. I consider it so important to make sure Eric understands that *who* he is as a person is, to a certain degree, separate from what he does. In other words, just because he does something "bad" doesn't mean he's a "bad" boy.

Children shouldn't be labeled. They're still learning. If we label them, we're essentially telling them who they're destined to become. If I told Eric that he was "bad" every time he did something wrong, I guarantee that he'd begin to believe it! And if he believes that he's a bad boy, he's going to act like a bad boy. It benefits him to understand that it is possible for a good boy to make a mistake and do a bad thing but still be considered a good boy. The key is that *good* boys will learn from their mistakes and make the necessary changes.

I have just one other discipline-oriented pet peeve that I'd like to share: the empty threat. I've been guilty of this from time to time despite my best intentions. An empty threat might go something like this: "If you don't behave, we're never going to Grandma's house again!" It's a threatened punishment that, for obvious reasons, will not be followed through with. The only way that this specific threat would be carried out is if the entire family was willing to sacrifice their relationship with Grandma in the name of the punishment! Most likely, that would not be the case. Therefore this threat is no more than a scare tactic.

I'm certain that Eric won't take me seriously for long if I use scare tactics or words that I can't live up to like "never" and "always" in a punishment. He's not the only one, as most children will quickly catch on to the fact that this type of punishment threat is meaningless. Children aren't stupid. So, since this is one form of discipline that will not produce the desired result of obedience, we may as well not use it at all. After all, there are plenty of effective alternatives.

I've had enough of discipline for now - not in real life, of course, just in this book. It's a necessary evil of a child's character development, but it's not much fun, so I'll gladly move on to a facet of character about which I can really get enthused: enthusiasm (no pun intended).

Just out of curiosity – do you consider life to be a miracle or an annoyance? What about motherhood? Do you consider that to be a joy or a bother? There is no right or wrong answer to either of these questions. In fact, chances are that your answers will be markedly different at different times. I know that mine are. The point that I'm trying to make with these questions is that each one of us has a choice as to how we will look at things at any given point in time. Undoubtedly, there's a lot of bad stuff that happens in our world, but we each have a choice as to whether or not we focus on that bad stuff. Not surprisingly, I find that when I choose to focus mostly on positives I tend to get excited and enthusiastic, whereas when I place more focus on the negatives I quickly become depressed and gloomy.

Wouldn't it be cool if we all could view the world through the eyes of a child? Wait - we can! The reality is that we don't always have to teach our children - they can also teach us. They can teach us how to see the world from a point-of-view that is still naïve to the "too-much-information-age" - a very positive point-of-view indeed! And, not only do we learn from our kids while we do this, but we also inadvertently show support for their enthusiastic, rose-colored-glasses views. As with anything we practice, eventually positive thinking will become a habit. It really is just another choice that we make.

For those of you who may be questioning my theory on positive thinking due to your fear of having your kids grow up blind to the evils of the world, and therefore weak, unsuspecting, and vulnerable, please rest assured that I'm not suggesting that we ignore the fact that bad stuff happens. After all, it does. It's just that we are in control of how much consideration we give to the bad stuff. This is a big challenge for me (and for the media, obviously). On one hand, I am very positive and enthusiastic. On the other hand, and as I pointed out earlier in this book, I can be rather anxious, worrisome and overly concerned with the bad stuff. I'm trying desperately not to pass this anxious side of myself on to Eric, but unfortunately I'm beginning to think that this may be an inborn trait and therefore somewhat out of my control. It really seems that, no matter what I say or do or how I react in front of him, Eric becomes worrisome and anxious with even the slightest trigger. I don't know – maybe this is just the work of instinct. Yes, frightening as it may seem, it does make sense to me that Eric can pick up on my true feelings, despite my best effort at pretending that I am not scared when I am, or not worried when I am (especially since I've already established that my acting skills aren't even close to being worthy of Hollywood!).

Well, I suppose I'll be satisfied as long as anxiety and worry don't completely wipe out Eric's energy and enthusiasm. I want so badly for him to feel excited about his life, his family, and his accomplishments. I mean, why not get excited about all of that? Life is not going to be perfect. That's a fact. And although I want Eric to be prepared to face sadness or disappointment when it occurs … and it will occur … I know that staying focused on the positives will actually help him to see positive things *within* the negatives, in turn making the negatives seem ... well ... less negative!

Is there an official term for the choice between adopting a positive point-of-view or a negative point-of-view? Yes. It's called "perspective." I could spend pages and pages on this concept. It is a constantly changing variable that perfectly illustrates the role of *experience* with regard to character building.

My perspective has already changed many times throughout my life as a result of my experiences. I notice this with elderly people – today they may take a certain situation with a grain of salt that, many years earlier, would have been devastating to them. Why? Because of experience. It is likely that an older person has survived through a variety of situations of so many different severity levels, that their perspective changes regarding what they consider to be bad or, on the flip side, not so bad. It sure is a shame that we can't mix the wisdom of the elderly with the enthusiasm of the very young. What a joyful individual that would make!

I'll never forget my most memorable lesson in "perspective" to date. It came from my husband and his dear mother (although Gary's mother insists she can't take the credit, so it might very well be a Gary-original!) Their favorite response after something doesn't go as well as expected is "best I could do." Well, the first time I heard Gary say that I figured that he definitely must be an underachiever. I had never considered him lazy, but I pondered whether a man who was so easy on himself would actually make a good husband. Chances were I'd be supporting him for the rest of our lives, bringing home the bacon *and* frying it up in the pan. After all, I could not relate to that statement. Is it ever "the best I could do?" No. If I faltered, it meant that I just didn't give it my best - no one to blame but myself, so I should be punished. I deserved to be angry at myself for being less than perfect. Not exactly a productive viewpoint, but one that I once claimed as my own.

Then it dawned on me. Gary and his mom were right. When I do something, even if it doesn't appear to be my one-hundred percent best effort, it is still the best I can do at that specific point in time. One hundred percent effort means giving the one hundred percent that I have available to me at the time. I can be sick, anxious or tired and still give something my all, but the results may not be quite as good as they would have been on a better day. So, instead of assuming that this phrase could be the slogan for the National Association of Lazy People, I'm now okay with its true meaning: the world is not perfect, nor am I. Not only did my newfound understanding provide a lesson in perspective, but it was also proof that perspective does, in fact, change constantly. With any luck Gary and his mom will help Eric grasp this concept at a very young age!

It's true that the perspective I choose affects my life, not to mention the lives of those around me, especially that of my family. And it's hard to deny my chosen perspective when Eric is right by my side, very willing to imitate the tone and content of whatever I say or do. I can't emphasize enough how important it is for Eric to adopt the perspective that there is a positive to be found within every negative. This idea actually refers to what has been termed by Dr. Robert Schuller as "possibility thinking": believing and finding a way to accomplish something, even when it seems impossible or others tell you that you can't do it. Dr. Schuller has written many books on this way of thinking, prompting me and countless others to prescribe to the belief that should really be, in my opinion, common sense.

The truth is, anyone who is successful in any endeavor prescribes to possibility thinking, whether they realize it or not. Most often, when a successful person encounters a roadblock or experiences a letdown, rather than accept it as a negative, he or she finds a way to turn it into a positive. Perhaps this skill comes naturally to some. Not to me. It will be well worth the time and effort that it is taking me to master it, however. I am certain that this perspective, once adopted, will lead to greater happiness and contentment.

What will happen if I choose not to prescribe to possibility thinking? For one, I definitely won't reach my goals if I succumb to every roadblock or run in the opposite direction whenever difficulty arises along the way. And if I don't reach my desired goals, I will always wonder "what if?" What if I had continued to move forward despite the doubts of others? What if I had realized my full potential rather than giving up halfway through because of my own fear of failure? I consider a "what if" to be something that I really wanted to do at some point in my life, but, for some reason I have not done it. Perhaps somewhere along the way I followed someone else's advice, or listened to someone else's doubts, rather than following my own heart. I may have based my academic or career choices on someone else's opinion rather than on my own desires. Maybe I've made certain decisions in my life solely because I felt that the alternative wasn't attainable based on my current level of income, knowledge, or some other factor. Those are the types of experiences that result in "what ifs."

I'm not a fan of "what ifs" and therefore I would really like to help Eric to limit them in his own life. Don't get me wrong; I know that, realistically, we all will have a few of them to deal with, simply because there are truly no guarantees in life. I think the saddest "what if," however, is one resulting from a decision not to shoot for a dream - not taking the risk, but instead playing it safe, leaving one to wonder if an idea could ever have worked.

I want Eric to understand early on that *he* is the only person who can decide what he can or can't accomplish. He also needs to realize that some goals will be more difficult than others to attain and there *will* be disappointments along the way, but even the longest journey begins with the first step. A possibility-oriented attitude, along with parental support in helping him determine what steps to take to have the best chance to reach his goals, will be precursors to his success and happiness.

I'll be honest - I have never dealt well with disappointment, especially when it comes to losing a competition. Ask any of my friends or family members or anybody who has ever seen me compete, and they will support this claim. I was really hoping that I could prevent this painful quality of mine from invading Eric's genetic makeup. Well, I must say that we have been blessed with an extremely competitive, winning-oriented, young man whose genetic makeup was, no doubt, invaded in a big way! I don't mean to make this trait sound all bad – in fact, it *could* turn out to be an incredibly good thing, but only if channeled properly.

Unfortunately in my case, a competitive nature, or rather my own version of it, has been my own worst enemy. My failure to see the point of taking on a challenge if it cannot be won has been my downfall! As a result of this tendency, I became mentally useless as soon as I began to fall behind in pretty much any competition. I have vowed that I will not let this happen to my son, although once again I'm learning that I may have to surrender to the role of genes (or, perhaps, instinct) in this case and, like I said, just try to help Eric channel this potentially nasty force in a positive direction.

Actually, Gary and I have already begun to take certain steps to help teach Eric to use his competitive nature to his advantage. We are trying to emphasize the "it's a journey, not a destination" perspective. We want him to rise to any challenge and not give up just because he is not the best at something or because he may be taking longer than others to learn something. I figure that if he participates in a game or competition with his main intention being to learn from it, he will follow it through to completion, win or lose. We've got our work cut out for us, because, even at this early stage of life, Eric often wants to quit when he's losing a game. Sure, to a degree, this is just a kid being a kid. But we still don't let him quit. If we let him quit now when things aren't going his way, I'm afraid that will become an easy way out for him as he gets older.

I wish that all of us could have the attitude that it's worth playing the game whether we are winning or not. Speaking of that, there's a great Blue's Clues video out there that does a really good job of stressing the importance of not giving up. It's called "Blue's Big Musical Adventure." If you haven't seen this one, you should check it out. Basically, Blue and Steve are putting together a musical show for all of their friends. While on stage, some of the characters mess up and forget their lines and, as a result, want to quit. Steve and all the friends encourage them with a song that emphasizes never giving up. "Don't give up, just go on" is the chorus of the song, which I think does a great job of driving the point home to young children.

Giving up is one thing, but a child changing his mind is another thing altogether. Eric is still very young. He should be able to experiment with different activities until he finds the ones that he really enjoys. He may start out playing soccer but then decide it's not really his "thing" so he'll stop playing and move on to something different. I don't consider that quitting, unless, of course, a pattern begins to develop where there is an obvious correlation between losing or disappointment, and loss of interest in an activity. That would then seem to reflect a need to win issue and that *is* quitting. It's a fine line but it's so important for Eric just to be a kid, so I'm hoping not to overreact and jump to negative conclusions every time he wants to switch gears by trying something different.

An important concept that goes hand-in-hand with possibility thinking is goal-setting. Everybody needs to have goals, even young kids. Short- and long-term goals provide us all with a sense of purpose. I'm not talking about complex, difficult goals, but rather simple, everyday goals. One of my short-term goals, for example, is sitting and talking with Eric while he eats his after-school snack. As you might imagine, this isn't a goal that I have to work hard to achieve – catching up on what happened during his day is something that I want to do and that I enjoy doing. In fact, the only reason that I've acknowledged this as a "goal" is because it is a big step toward achieving my very important long-term goal of establishing and maintaining open communication with Eric. You see, I'm hoping that, with our snack session atop my list of daily priorities throughout his entire school experience, it will eventually become automatic for him to share his daily experiences with me.

Long-term goals are made up of various smaller, short-term goals that can be as specific or general as you want them to be. For instance, Eric may have the long-term goal of learning the zero through ten addition facts by the summer, while I may have the long-term goal of becoming a more tolerant parent. My goal is relatively general, so I'll not only need to define what "more tolerant" actually means to me, but I also must identify lots of little, detailed steps on how to get there. Eric's goal is more specific – not only is its meaning clear, but it is also relatively apparent what he'll have to do to achieve it. Overall, the more specific the goal, the easier it is to plan for and ultimately attain.

This brings me back to the end product of goal-setting: development of a sense of purpose. Feeling as though I have a purpose in life helps me remain on a positive track and not stray into self-destructive areas. Similarly, I believe if Eric develops a sense of purpose early in his life, it will lessen the chances that he will make poor choices that may work against him as he gets older. Setting some small goals, even now, will keep him interested in and enthusiastic about his life with less self-doubt and confusion, and with increased feelings of self-worth.

I have found that the act of helping others also creates a feeling of purpose in my life. We all can be guilty of taking what we have for granted and living in our own comfortable little cocoon at times, even if we don't mean to. Helping those less fortunate than ourselves is an acknowledgment that everyone matters and an important lesson that I want Eric to learn. In fact, I would like him to eventually consider this to be the most important use of his time. Already, I notice that he follows my lead when he witnesses me helping others. So even though it may be difficult, at least right now, for him to imagine that there are people in our world who don't have food to eat, a house to live in, or cool toys to play with, he can at least understand that it is always nice to give a little of what we have to somebody who doesn't have as much.

Another concept having to do with character that is sometimes quite difficult for young kids to understand is "The Golden Rule." Actually, this seems to cause quite a bit of conflict in the adult mind as well - it seems as though the old "eye for an eye" philosophy comes a little bit more naturally for many of us!

Gary and I had the opportunity to address this complex little rule with Eric pretty early on, specifically in response to a bullying issue he faced. Not surprisingly, Eric's account of his reaction to the bully went something like this: "But Mommy, he was mean to me so I was mean back!" When we tried to explain to him that we should treat people the same way that we want them to treat us, *regardless* of how they actually treat us, he looked at us as though we had lost our minds! I'm guessing that we'll have to be patient while teaching Eric this lesson!

There are far too many factors involved in "character" for me to expound upon individually, although, looking back at this chapter, I seem to have made a go of it. The truth is that different people have very different ideas regarding what is right and what is wrong or what is good and what is bad, and therefore they frequently have different thoughts on what defines good character versus what defines bad character. Although Gary and I are trying to instill in Eric the values and beliefs that *we* feel are right, as Eric grows up, he will begin to determine which of those values and beliefs are truly right for him. I hold the position that, as long as his belief system does not purposely inflict pain on others, he should hold true to that belief system. If he *does* hold true to his beliefs, he will have developed "strength of character," meaning that his beliefs will be strong enough to stick. I think this is where faith, or belief in a higher power, has some influence.

In order for me to have strength of character, there has to be some driving force behind my belief system, and often times that driving force is spirituality. Does spirituality represent yet another parental responsibility? Well, if Gary and I want Eric to explore spirituality and/or religion, I suppose that, yes, we must be the ones to lead the way. It sure would be a big help if society, in general, would support the open acknowledgment of a higher power, regardless of its name.

Honestly, I am totally appalled by the trend in society today to limit, or even eliminate, references to God in our schools or any other public domain. Where is the strength of character within our society? I think that everyone needs to have faith in some higher power, whether that's God or Allah or some other spiritual force. To try to ignore that or take that source of strength away sends a terrible message to kids. Faith and hope in a higher power give us strength when nothing else can. There is no doubt in my mind that spirituality is the energy behind character. Human beings need the strength provided by faith, or spirituality, to handle many of life's challenges. We are all touched, at one time or another, by loss of loved ones, tragedies of nature and illness. How do we get through it all? I know that I get through difficulties with prayer, fellowship of friends and neighbors, and belief that there is a greater, more powerful force watching over us.

If, at this point, you are thinking that I'm a religious person, you're wrong. Spiritual – yes; religious – no. In fact, Gary, Eric and I currently don't belong to an organized church or religious group, but we do believe in God. We say daily prayers and read portions of the Bible with Eric. He is very curious about the Bible; he has question after question, most of which neither Gary nor I can answer well enough. We've tried to explain Heaven and Hell, illness and death, and all of the "miracles" surrounding us to the best of our ability. Although we can't answer *all* of Eric's questions adequately, for right now we can at least try to provide him with a sense of positive spirituality. I want him to view God as a helpful, caring, loving force rather than something to be feared. I believe that, if he feels like he can turn to God for strength and understanding, nothing will seem insurmountable to him as he goes through his life. When he is sad or disappointed he'll know the difference between those situations that he can control or change and those that he cannot.

Gary, Eric and I happen to be Christians, we could just as easily be Jewish, Buddhist or Muslim. It doesn't matter what higher being we believe in. The key is that we believe in something, as long as that something is inherently good. As I mentioned earlier, our spirituality is especially helpful when situations occur that have no worldly explanation. Death is one example of that. Eric already has been exposed to the death of quite a few goldfish, his grandmother's dog and his great-grandfather. As I expected, these events have prompted tons of questions regarding mortality. Had it not been for the Bible, I'm not exactly sure how I would have answered all of his questions, because I haven't quite worked through my own issues with death. In fact, I'm not comfortable with that subject in the least (not that many people are). I'd much rather have the birds and bees discussion one thousand times than deal with the subject of death. So, not only does turning to the Bible for answers help Eric, but it also helps me. It helps me address the subject straight on and allow Eric to gain strength in the belief that death is not a bad thing but merely a rebirth into an even better place. As I know all too well, fear and anxiety about our constantly changing lives can be paralyzing. I would love for Eric to be able to live his life in acceptance of the ultimate end of *this* life, rather than in fear of it. I believe that the early development of deep spiritual roots will make that goal attainable.

~ 9 ~

The Sponge

There never was a woman like her. She was gentle as a dove and brave as a lioness... The memory of my mother and her teachings were, after all, the only capital I had to start life with, and on that capital I have made my way.
- ANDREW JACKSON

Kids are amazing. I can honestly say that I entered into motherhood naïve to the incredible brain capacity of young children. This was probably a good thing. I mean, I didn't have any expectations initially, so I didn't spend time worrying whether or not Eric would be smart or how much he could learn or when he should learn it. But, the funny thing is, I find that sometimes when I don't have any expectations, amazing things happen. In this case, for instance, our manner of "being there" for

Eric led to some learning-based results that Gary and I had not considered.

My road to accidentally discovering a child's huge capacity to learn all began quite innocently with my hatred ... no, "hatred" is too strong a word ... rather my lack of enthusiasm ... for the infant stage. After all, what can you do with a child who can't speak and has extremely limited physical ability? I found the infant stage boring, to say the least. All that I could do was worry endlessly, as new mothers sometimes do. Constantly checking Eric's breathing while he slept, making sure he wasn't exposed to germs (like I could control that), and keeping track of his growth patterns and the infamous percentiles - which started out on the high end of the scale then ended up on the low end, no thanks to my side of the family. Plus, *I* had just endured a huge change in *my* life – no more daily nine-to-five adult interaction since I placed my career on the back burner. Quite simply, I was in the midst of the reality that I was no longer my own main concern!

Woe was me? Not necessarily. There *was* one way that I could make the infant stage more exciting and less stressful for *me* and that was to find a way to communicate with Eric as I would a peer. So, I set out to accomplish the same thing with Eric as I had with Sigmund, the dog, just a few years earlier. I bestowed upon him a voice, opinions, and whatever else was necessary to allow me to interact with him on an adult level. Yes, I believed this was just what the infant stage needed to become exciting.

As I explained earlier, Eric and I discussed many issues throughout those initial, potentially non-communicative months. He had a very strong opinion on everything – from wall color to meal selection. We talked during diaper changes; we talked while we were nursing. Basically, we talked all the time. He never disagreed with me, since I provided all of the questions *and* all of the answers. This new method seemed to work very well, except when we were in the company of others. I suppose I shouldn't have been surprised that I would receive strange looks from innocent bystanders, especially the people at work (if you remember, at the time, my job was such that Eric could be with me at the office a few times per week). Although my door was often closed while Eric was with me at the office, it was quite common for curious coworkers to peek in upon hearing my voice in a seeming adult conversation, knowing that Eric was the only one in there with me! To their surprise, that's just who I was talking to - my infant son! Yes, I do have an active imagination and yes, it has proven to be helpful in my quest to avoid boredom.

As an infant, not only did Eric become accustomed to a lot of verbal interaction with me, but, as I described earlier, he also quickly became used to business meetings, phone calls and interruptions in general – sometimes at inopportune times. This was rather stressful for me, but it certainly helped both of us build patience. Eric's interaction with the bankers, customers and suppliers as well as his multitude of surrogate aunts and uncles (all of the employees of the company) during infancy definitely played a huge role in jumpstarting his communication and thinking skills. He had been exposed to situations within his first year of life to which most children may never be exposed. He truly was a part of my daily life, never having to be on the outside looking in, but rather right smack in the middle of the action, no matter if the "action" was good or bad, positive or negative. Although there were many times when I felt as though I was dragging him around too much, he seemed to enjoy himself and was a generally happy baby. At the time, though, I had no idea that there were so many additional benefits to our arrangement.

Eric began to communicate more and more throughout his first year, as most babies do. He seemed to be a sharp little guy, as he was learning the alphabet, numbers and even new words with ease. Of course neither Gary nor I had a barometer by which to judge the age-appropriateness of Eric's development, so we merely took for granted that he was on par with other kids his age. That is, until people began to comment. Now, it wasn't surprising when family members oogled over Eric's aptitude for his age, since family members tend to do that, whether or not such a reaction is warranted. But when non-family-members began to voice similar surprise, Gary and I took notice.

As Eric literally crawled around the office day after day, coworkers developed the habit of quizzing him on basic skills like letter and number recognition. Whenever he would answer their questions correctly, which happened more often than not, they would grin in disbelief and then continue to try to baffle him. It was actually quite amusing to watch! My cousin and fellow coworker took a special interest in Eric's knowledge. She was shocked at his ability to retain facts that she communicated to him in passing. As both a mother and a grandmother herself, she felt more than adequately qualified to label Eric's knowledge, so that is exactly what she did. She labeled it as age-*inappropriate* and believed it to be a direct result of Gary and my strange obsession with explaining things to Eric in great detail. My cousin was also quick to point out that, even when Eric was able to ask only broken questions, neither Gary nor I ever answered with the word "because." Believe me, I'd love to take credit for inventing this new method of communicating with children in order to help them gain knowledge at an early age, but the truth is, until my cousin pointed out some of our specific tendencies, neither Gary nor I had noticed what we were doing. Let's face it - we are the people who talk to our dog as though he is human. And clearly, it is our nature to explain things (some call it ramble) in great detail to whoever will listen. Of course we also hold the belief that it is our parental responsibility to answer Eric's questions. So, the bottom line is we have mostly our own idiosyncrasies to thank for many of these unforeseen benefits.

Admittedly, after listening to the comments and reactions of other people, I began to think more seriously about the effects of my communication with Eric. Also, out of curiosity, I began to pay more attention to the communication between other parents and their kids as well as their reactions to their kids' questions. Surprisingly, more often than not, parents didn't even bother to answer their children's questions! Sometimes the word "because" was used, but many times the kids' questions were just ignored. I'd like to think that these parents were not purposely being rude to their children. Perhaps some parents merely assume that their kids aren't likely to understand their answers, so there is no point in wasting their breath. If that's the case, I am in disagreement with their assumption.

Yet another situation occurred that made a big impression on Gary and me. When Eric was about six months old, we took a trip to the beach to visit my in-laws. Upon our arrival, a nearby friend of the family stopped in to meet Eric for the first time. I'll never forget the surprise on our friend's face when she began to interact with our son. She obviously wasn't expecting that Eric would carry on a mini-conversation with her, given his young age. "He's so smart! …. He's so aware!" she exclaimed. Gary and I were almost embarrassed by her rather extreme reaction, but she was genuinely dumbfounded by Eric's level of awareness and ability to communicate for his age.

There was no doubt to us that Eric appeared very aware, almost as though he was thinking all of the time, but why was this such a big deal? Well, after giving it much thought, I finally realized the significance: Eric is living proof that the infant stage *isn't* just a boring stage during which a child can't understand. In fact, perhaps it is actually the time when a child is *most* capable of learning. Perhaps this is when a child is *most* readily able to acquire the initial building blocks for understanding and thinking. And, if that's the case, communicating with an infant as though he *can* understand, whether he is actually able to or not, is a good thing. It is essential that we acknowledge that the mind of a young child is most similar to a sponge, and then act accordingly.

I hope that you understand that my intention is not to brag about Eric, nor is it my intention to definitively judge whether his skills and knowledge are age-inappropriate or not. You see, this isn't just about Eric; it's about every young child out there. I hold the belief that all young children can develop so-called "age-inappropriate" skills and capabilities, because they all have a huge capacity to learn. Unfortunately, I also believe that their great capacity to learn is often stifled, rather than nurtured, by their parents or guardians.

Whether or not the accidental "jump start" that Eric received early on will continue to impact his life positively remains to be seen. I do know for sure that he's stuck with a mom and dad whose idiosyncrasies far outnumber their formal parenting credentials, which makes it very likely that the manner in which we deal with him will not change any time soon. And if our manner of dealing with Eric is actually helping him learn, well then, that makes me very happy.

I am excited to say that my long list of accidental discoveries continues to grow with each new day. These discoveries necessitate flexibility on my part because their resulting lessons continually shape who I am and how I relate to Eric. An example of this is a specific discovery of ours that is related to "possibility thinking" from the last chapter.

When Eric was very young, Gary and I had our first chance to turn behavior that we initially considered to be negative into a positive learning experience for all involved: Eric's tendency to dawdle during dinner. Yes, one of Eric's biggest issues has been his hatred of mealtimes, which continues to this day. He didn't have a problem with eating when he was being nursed or bottle-fed, but as soon as we introduced baby food, mealtime became something that he had neither the time nor the patience to endure.

After a few frustrating months of spending a couple of hours – yes, a couple of hours - each night trying to persuade Eric to eat his dinner, Gary and I decided to approach the issue from a different perspective. In order to get Eric to eat, we'd attempt to make the experience more fun for him. We'd play games, sneak a bite into his mouth, sing songs, sneak a bite into his mouth, and so on. We had no choice. We had to get food into his little body, and we knew that going ballistic would likely have the opposite effect, especially at Eric's young age. Still, it took all we had NOT to lose our patience.

One of Eric's favorite distractions during mealtime was his magnetic doodling board. What a great toy! He could draw on the screen and then push a lever to wipe it clean and start over. It was very simplistic, and allowed us to play little games that Eric enjoyed and that seemed to spark his love of learning. Alphabet and number games along with reading and writing practice all became part of our mealtime repertoire. Eric learned letters, numbers, basic addition and subtraction, the fifty United States in alphabetical order as well as various other facts, figures and songs while he was at the dinner table. He was learning a lot of cool stuff and, eventually, he even began to eat his meals without complaining! That was our first tangible experience with possibility thinking – we now had proof that not all things that we think are totally negative actually are, as there are lessons to be learned and benefits to be gained from every situation. The struggle to get Eric to eat was won through creativity and distraction. From an eating habit standpoint, we may have done some damage. From a learning and quality time standpoint, this definitely was a key time, unintentionally.

Gary and I certainly learned a lot about kids and parenting through our own idiosyncrasies. Of course there are a multitude of books out there that emphasize an infant's capacity to learn and how to best take advantage of that. Perhaps reading those books would have been a bit easier than learning by accident, but it may not have been as much fun.

The truth is, when I eventually realized just how much knowledge Eric could retain at such a young age, I felt that another phase of my own redefinition had begun. Through my new discoveries, it became even clearer that my goal of making a difference in this world was definitely going to come to fruition by giving Eric the necessary tools and confidence so that *he* could make a positive difference in this world. Wow.

How true it is that salary, belongings, career status, and anything related to those things really are not what *my* success will be based on. No, instead, my success will be judged by my son's overall happiness, character and sense of security. He's got an incredible amount of potential and a lifetime to let it develop. Once I realized how much information Eric was capable of absorbing, I vowed that I would become purposeful in continuing to do those things that, until this point, I was doing unintentionally. Uh-oh!

Why the "uh-oh"? Well, as you might imagine based on what I've revealed about my own personality so far, I tend to be an extremist - maybe obsessive-compulsive too; definitely competitive. Nevertheless, my latest discovery - that a young child's brain can be likened to a sponge - came with a price: my own self-imposed pressure to keep Eric intellectually stimulated one hundred percent of the time while making sure to foster his love of learning.

My mind raced. How could such a general, though intense, long-term goal be broken down into a meaningful and manageable set of short-term goals? I was certain about one thing: I must figure out the answer quickly so that "training" could commence immediately, as these goals would be easiest to achieve prior to Eric's contact with the outside world (school, specifically). Enter teachers and peers and I'd have an even bigger challenge on my hands.

Understand that, although I've always attempted to give one-hundred percent to my goals throughout my life, this would be slightly different. This goal would literally be a full-time job; a new lifestyle. Not only that, but it would be essential that I contain my own need for perfection while pursuing this one. This time I couldn't possibly expect all wins and no losses. This time I must not allow myself to fall apart with the smallest setback or with the slightest mistake. Obviously *that* perspective had not worked to my benefit in the past, probably because perfection doesn't exist in our world. In this case, though, not only would it be impossible to be perfect, but I wouldn't have total control of the outcome because I would not be the only person influencing Eric's perspective.

Now that you're probably concerned by my extreme reaction to my newfound goals, I must reassure you. You see, I'm happy to say that I realized, just in the nick of time, that I would drive myself (and everyone else) crazy with my idea to intellectually stimulate Eric all the time. This time I could proudly say that I was successful in taking the offensive against my tendency to obsess over, and ultimately ruin, a good thing.

I reached the conclusion that, since Eric had managed to learn just fine up to that point, it really would be pointless for us to change what we had been doing all along. I figured out that, if kids truly are sponges, they will soak up information that is presented to them quite naturally and effortlessly, without the transformation of Mommy into *Sergeant* Mommy. Also, it wouldn't be long until Eric would be off to preschool for a couple of mornings a week, anyway. I wanted to spend our time together enjoying each other, not worrying about whether or not Eric's brain was being filled with challenging stimuli from dawn until dusk. I knew that would take care of itself.

Again, I can't emphasize enough that it is often when you have no expectations that amazing things happen. Eric and I had a great time just chilling out together before the structured schedule of preschool began. We both needed that.

~ 10 ~

School Days

The mother-child relationship is paradoxical and, in a sense, tragic. It requires the most intense love on the mother's side, yet this very love must help the child grow away from the mother, and to become fully independent.
- ERICH FROMM

You'll be happy to know that I did, in fact, manage to stick to my less-obsessive plan of chilling out and having fun with Eric during that last summer of toddlerhood. We played and talked, and talked and played. Time truly flies when you are having fun. The infant stage flew, the toddler stage flew, and now Eric was three-and-a-half years old and on the brink of entering preschool!

I was concerned. Many of Eric's peers had been in daycare or some sort of program outside of their home and apart from their mommies prior to this first school experience. Not Eric. Come to think of it, had I not been there myself, I wouldn't be able to say for sure that the doctor actually cut the umbilical cord at birth. Not that it really mattered, until now. I naturally *assumed* (don't you love my clever use of the word "assumed" as a cover-up for that nasty word - "expected"?) that all of those other kids would have an easier time adjusting to preschool than Eric would (or I, for that matter). How could that not be the case, since Eric and I had been together almost every waking moment of his life so far?

Alright, I was also nervous because *my* memories of going to school for the first time were not so good. I cried incessantly as the school bus approached on my own first day of school. It was really hard for me to adjust, but, as I've come to find out and can now imagine quite easily, it was even harder for my mom. She had no choice but to make me go to school even though I was an emotional mess. Needless to say, she worried about me all morning long while I was away.

I knew that if Eric's reaction to his first day of school was at all similar to mine, I would be in trouble. I knew that it wouldn't take much for me to just let him skip preschool altogether and resort to a lifetime of homeschooling and online degree programs. Although that wouldn't necessarily be a bad thing, I figured that, for now, it would be better to keep all of our options open.

So, Eric and I began to talk about his upcoming school experience over and over again many months in advance. Not only that, but we trekked in and out of a multitude of preschools and early learning centers, trying to find the perfect fit for both of us. I held this decision at the highest level of importance, knowing that Eric's first experience with school would likely shape his entire long-term perspective. How ironic that it was a cool playground that led us to our destiny.

It was definitely meant to be. I'll never forget it. Eric and I were driving to the grocery store one day, as we had many, many times before. This time, however, I happened to take better notice of a rather large daycare center that we passed on the right hand side of the road, tucked back a bit. The first thing that struck me about the place was that it had a great playground – a wooden train, a cool swing-set and a bunch of other fun stuff all grouped together in a cozy-looking, partially wooded area. Unfortunately, this facility was much too big to house a preschool with the small class size for which we were looking. It was such a serene setting, though, that I couldn't get it out of my mind. So, despite my doubts, I decided to return on another day to check out the place more thoroughly.

Out of utter curiosity and the fact that we had nothing to lose by doing so, we did return a few days later to find out more. To my surprise, not only did this "huge" center have a preschool, but the class size was limited to ten kids, something almost unheard of amongst the other schools we had visited! I couldn't believe it! We met the director, who showed us the preschool classroom and even introduced us to the teacher – a very kind, enthusiastic, middle-aged woman whose love of children was immediately obvious. Clearly this was not what we had expected. Clearly, this preschool was *the one*!

With Eric's enthusiastic support, I formally enrolled him in the Tuesday morning/Thursday morning class set to begin in the fall, only a few short months away. Of course, those months passed quickly and were filled with conversation after conversation about any potential fears and concerns that Eric had. As a result of our mental preparation, we both were relatively calm and somewhat reassured by the time the initial day of school arrived.

The first day of preschool came and went without any major issues or trauma. I wiped the sweat from my brow and breathed a sigh of relief. So far anyway, it seemed as though we had made the right choice. Admittedly, my fear that being a full-time stay-at-home mom to Eric would somehow make this a more difficult adjustment for him was for naught. I think it is safe to say that the disposition of Eric's teacher, Mrs. Schroeder, contributed to this positive outcome.

From the get-go Mrs. Schroeder and I seemed to hold a similar philosophy regarding kids. Just as I feel that it is my job to unconditionally support and encourage Eric to pursue his interests and to be the best he can be, so too did Mrs. Schroeder consider that her job. I have no doubt that this helped to insure Eric's smooth transition. And because Eric and I had talked nonstop about his feelings for about six months – his fear of being away from me, his anxiety that he may not meet friends in his class, and also any excitement he felt - he knew that it was okay to have all of those feelings, both positive and negative, and he knew he wasn't the only one to have them. He was actually surprised to discover that his fears about the impending preschool experience were much worse than the experience itself. Wow! What a helpful lesson to learn at such a young age!

Now that Eric had become an official preschooler, I wasn't expecting time to give me any break by slowing down, and I was right - it flew, as usual. Eric and I spent quality time together at home on Mondays, Wednesdays and Fridays, and I attempted to run errands, work out and write during school hours on Tuesday and Thursday mornings. It was relatively easy to keep my finger on the pulse of Eric's life at that point, as his teacher did a wonderful job of sharing the events and excitement of each day with all of the parents. I took advantage of every available opportunity to help out at school with holiday parties, field trips and class picnics. I couldn't have been happier with the experience. Eric had a fantastic first year – not only was Mrs. Schroeder great, but the class was made up of a really nice group of children. It was evident by year-end that Eric had come out of his shell quite a bit. He truly enjoyed his time at school and it was obvious that he was benefiting socially from the experience. Preschool was good for me too, as it provided me with a nice, slow transition to get used to not having Eric around all the time

The first year of preschool quickly turned into the second. Now Monday mornings, Wednesday mornings and Friday mornings were all mine – another manageable, though significant, change. With three mornings per week now open, I began to think about part-time employment. Obviously, working while Eric was at school would not cut into my time with my son and therefore would not interfere with my commitment to being a stay-at-home mom. Or would it? After all, it was very important to me to continue to participate in school activities – something that would be next to impossible to do with a job. Well, for good reason, that sudden revelation was all that was needed to squelch my part-time employment idea. Thank goodness. Once again, Eric and I couldn't have been happier. He looked forward to my participation in special events, and greeting me at the classroom door at the end of each school day. We have lasting memories from that special time and I shudder to think what I would have missed had I returned to work just then.

If you've grown tired of hearing about my intense desire to stop time, I must apologize, because I am about to address this subject just once more (at least that is my intention). Can you really blame me though? After all, at the rate that time was progressing, not only would it soon be time for Eric to start Kindergarten, but I may as well consider renaming this book "I Am Grandmom!" And don't I have the right to mourn the fact that, once a kindergartner,

Eric would be at the mercy of the outside world for good and have no need for me anymore? (At least that was my perception.)

Although I felt confident that, by the end of this second year of preschool, Eric would be fully prepared to take the next step, I couldn't help but cringe every time I thought about it. For that reason I became even more thankful for our preschool experience - it provided Eric with a safe setting in which he could learn concepts like socialization, adaptation, compromise and sharing, not to mention economic and cultural diversity – things that would be difficult for us to teach him on our own. In fact, Gary and I didn't actually enroll Eric in preschool to master academics, although we realized that letters, numbers and miscellaneous academic-oriented subjects would be covered. We believed that, while Eric was very young and even before he entered school, it was our parental responsibility to provide Eric with a good understanding of the academic basics. I will explain my reasoning.

First, the toddler and preschool years are filled with tons of changes for these little people. Between learning some degree of independence and learning the social skills necessary to interact with other human beings, kids' time and energy in preschool is pretty much used up. The total meltdowns that are fairly common in the classroom at this level can be viewed as proof of this. The kids get tired and frustrated, and would rather play freely than participate in highly structured learning activities. Now I'm not suggesting that academics should be eliminated from the preschool curriculum, however I feel that parents can do the best job of building the initial foundation to nurture their kids' enjoyment of learning.

It was our experience that Eric's familiarity with the alphabet and numbers prior to entering preschool took a lot of the pressure off of him in that area once he got there. Not only that, but since the belief that learning is fun had been engrained in Eric since he was an infant, a negative preschool experience would not likely have squelched his enthusiasm in that regard. On the flip side, I believe that without a positive foundation, a negative preschool experience could have had a lasting negative impact. It is my hope that Eric will continue to view academics as more fun than work. I will always consider myself partially responsible for helping him maintain a passion for learning.

Eric's second year of preschool passed as quickly as his first and was just as positive an experience. The final days of that second year were approaching when Eric received an invitation to attend Kindergarten orientation at his future elementary school. Unfortunately, my little guy was scared stiff about this next step - so much so that he requested that we refer to Kindergarten as "big K" just so he didn't have to hear the actual word. I wished that I could take away all of his fears and, at the same time, overcome all of mine. I had no doubt, though, that we'd be able to work through our myriad of Kindergarten fears and concerns just as we did our preschool fears and concerns. All it would take would be the preparation, communication and being there to which we had already become accustomed. Once again, we would lay all of our feelings out on the table and talk about them until we were blue in the face or until all fear and doubt disappeared – whichever happened first.

Thankfully, "big K" orientation went relatively smoothly, with Eric's most outspoken fear being the "practice" school bus ride. Not only was this Eric's main anxiety-laden focus leading up to the orientation, but I came to find out that it was literally a source of panic for him *during* orientation (due mostly to a major faux pas on my part, unfortunately.) You see, I had incorrectly informed Eric that this short "test" ride would consist of a five-minute stint around the school driveway. Unbeknownst to me, the bus ride also included a short drive off of school property onto some local roads. Oh well. This was a good time to try out that new motto of mine: "Best I could do!" Needless to say, Eric survived my mistaken assumption and eventually calmed down. All it took was a reward trip to McDonald's and a heartfelt Mommy apology.

As we closed in on yet another stage of development, I acknowledged, once again, that the first five years of Eric's life had passed in a flash. Just when I had finally gotten used to one stage, another one seemed to jump up behind me and wack me over the head! Clearly, I wasn't the only one who felt this way. Brody's mom, Heidi, shared her feelings with me one day after dropping we dropped our boys off at preschool. She, too, had been feeling sad about the passage of time and the approaching end of Brody's preschool experience. As we shared our mutual dread, I went on to describe the ups and downs of Eric's Kindergarten orientation experience. I explained my feelings and fears in great detail, secretly hoping that she might offer some kind of anecdote to lessen my suffering. She did just that.

Heidi shared with me that she was watching Brody sleep one night not too long ago, when she finally admitted to herself that she had been wasting precious time. Although she realized all along that she couldn't possibly stop Brody from growing up, she continued to spend her time trying to do just that. So, from that point on, instead of wasting even more time attempting to prevent the inevitable, she decided that she would spend her time finding ways to be a better mother to him as he grows.

Truthfully, before Heidi shared her experience, it had never crossed my mind to look at the situation from that perspective. I'd been wasting precious time battling "time" in a knockdown, drag-out fight for five years, despite knowing, unquestionably, that I could never win! Well, not anymore. I knew that I couldn't go back and make the past any better nor could I eliminate regrets that I had or mistakes that I'd made. What I *could* do was make improvements for the future and eliminate any regrets that were yet to come. Just that quickly, I made a very important decision. Thanks Heidi, for putting this in perspective for me.

Shockingly, I was overcome by a general feeling of happiness during those last few days of preschool, probably because I had finally begun to loosen my grip on time and also focus more on the positives. I was still amazed at the fact that this wonderful preschool experience was the result of acting on a mere gut feeling. It's true that I've learned many lessons as a result of listening, or not, to what my heart is telling me, but this experience in doing so was the most significant. I couldn't help but imagine how differently things may have turned out had I passed by that cozy little playground without looking back. Honestly, I don't see how we could've been any better off under different circumstances. Eric (and I) both met so many truly special people, some of whom have undoubtedly become long-term friends. And of course I'll never forget Eric's teacher, Mrs. Schroeder, who celebrated each child's personality and their special talents. Because of her, Eric and the rest of the children emerged from their initial school experience feeling good about themselves and proud of their accomplishments, no matter how big or small. The atmosphere that she created in her classroom was ideal for Eric. Thank you so much, Mrs. Schroeder.

Needless to say, tears were flowing as Gary and I proudly watched Eric receive his preschool diploma on one beautiful morning late in May. Although this end of the year graduation party was cause for much celebration, it was also time to bid farewell to some of the people we met along the way and vow to keep in touch with others.

There were a lot of changes in the wind, but one thing would remain constant: my involvement in Eric's life. Another stage of development was gone, but Eric's need for me was not, nor would it ever be. I could choose to stand on the sidelines or get right in the game. The latter will always be my choice.

~ 11 ~

The Question

Children are the living messages we send to a time we will not see.
- JOHN W. WHITEHEAD

A very good friend of mine, who also happens to be the stay-at-home mom of two wonderful young boys, expressed concern to me one day that she hadn't accomplished anything significant in her life to date. "What have I done?" she asked. I had to resist my urge to answer her question, quickly realizing, of course, that she wasn't actually looking for my answer. Then she followed up with "What do I have to show for my life so far?" That was it. I could no longer resist. I proceeded to ramble (some would say "explain in great detail") about *my* perspective on what she had done in her life. Of course, all I had to do was think of her two boys and reflect on all that I knew she had done for them so far, with much more still to come. Her boys are nice, well-behaved and, most importantly, happy. From my perspective, she has been a great mother to them – they couldn't ask for better.

Like my friend, I've also had those occasional "what have I done?" moments when I suddenly long to be defined by some measurable accomplishment. Obviously, when a woman becomes a stay-at-home mom, all measurable achievements like corporate positions or salary levels are pretty much placed on hold. It's unfortunate that we sometimes fall into the trap of thinking that if we're not being paid to do something, then we're not actually doing something! I suppose wages and titles validate our performance, whereas the absence of wages and titles makes it difficult to evaluate not only what we're doing, but also how well we're doing it. And without a salary level or position, comparison to others is pretty much impossible. You can easily measure things like net worth, material accumulation, community status or career status and compare them to that of everyone else. I believe, however, that the *truly* important accomplishments in life cannot be measured so easily. In fact, I'll go so far as to say that, if an accomplishment of mine can be definitively measured, chances are it probably will not make or break my happiness in the long run.

Think of all of those things that can't be measured.. Are you a good mom? Who knows? What is a good mom? What does a good mom do? How many things does a good mom get done in a day? If Eric gets into trouble or has difficulty in school, does that mean I'm a bad mom? How do you ever measure that?

There is one definitive way that I can measure what I have done and how well I have done it up to this point: <u>smiles</u>. That's right. I believe the one and only measurement of my success as a mommy is how often Eric smiles. I realize that he will experience plenty of bumps and bruises along the way, and many of my mommy decisions will be second-guessable, but I must always ask myself "is Eric generally happy?"

I'm going to go out on a limb and say that it is a more difficult accomplishment to ensure my son's happiness than it is to earn a million bucks or get some highly-sought-after corporate position. I must wind and weave through ups and downs, over rough roads and disappointments, and generally walk a fine line between enclosing Eric in a cocoon and allowing him to fly alone in the open sky. My every reaction, my every emotion, my every habit or behavior is witnessed by this little person in training. Not only that, but no two kids are the same, not even within the same family, so each one likely reacts differently than the next. As a mom, I must be a psychologist, a teacher, a nurse, a housekeeper . . . the list goes on and on. Being a mom is a lot of pressure, but it is also loads of fun and the rewards are immeasurable!

Whenever I find myself questioning what I have done with my life so far, I know that it's time for me to pay better attention to the lives I am directly, and indirectly, affecting. I must acknowledge that when Eric is grown and no longer needs me to be at his beck and call, chances are that I'll miss the "good old days" and willingly give back all of my quantifiable achievements for the opportunity to return to his childhood.

An experience that I had not too long ago provides a great illustration of my point. Eric and I were outside playing together – it was a typical spring day for us, although I recall that it was also one our first experiences together without the stressors of my full-time job. I encouraged Eric to go next door to play with the little boy who is exactly his age and who also happened to be playing outside. Eric looked at me and, in a rather definitive tone, said "No, I'd rather play with you right now, Mommy!" That sentence really hit a chord. Not only did it make me feel special and incredibly important as Eric's mommy, but it also led me to reflect on the rush that we parents are sometimes in to get our kids out into the world and independent. I was especially guilty of this during the infant stage, when sleepless nights and multi-tasking days seemed overwhelming and were more the rule than the exception.

In the midst of my reflection, I realized that it won't be too long until I'd be wishing that Eric would *want* to spend time with me rather than wondering *why* he won't play with the neighborhood kids. At that point I'll want this time back for reliving, but that won't be possible.

So I smiled at my son, placed my garden tools carefully on the table, and erased all self-imposed household deadlines from my mind. I picked up the wiffle ball and gave it my best throw. If I have any regrets in my life, this was not going to be one of them. Eric hit the ball out of my reach, and then ran to give me a big hug. Each new day seemed to provide me with a lesson in appreciating time.

What have I done with my life? I don't really know yet. I can tell you what I am doing, but I cannot yet tell you "what I have done." What do I have to show for my life? That one's easy. When my redefinition took place more than five years ago, I got in the back seat, with Gary beside me there. Eric got into the front seat. It has been from the back seat that much of my fear has turned into excitement. It has been from the back seat that I have come to the realization that success is defined by the size of Eric's smile.

Right now, I see my little guy running around, happy to be alive, taking in the sights and sounds of the earth, appreciating the unknown and longing for more knowledge. I try to give him what knowledge I have and I try to feed off of his enthusiasm. He is a joy in our world. He has become a sensitive, caring little man. He blows me kisses from across the room and tells me he loves me every chance he gets. He gives us the gift of unconditional love and acceptance and has given us a lesson in expressing the same. I pray to God every night that Eric continues to be comfortable, safe, and happy.

That is what I have to show for my life. In measurable terms, I am most certainly a millionaire! I am the president of my own corporation! I am a General in the army! No, even better - I am Mommy.

About the Author

Susan Hughes lives in Pottstown, Pennsylvania with her husband Gary, their son Eric, and a myriad of pets including Sigmund, the coolest poodle ever. Prior to beginning her dream career as Mom to Eric, Sue received both a Bachelor's Degree in Psychology and a Master of Science degree in Education from Old Dominion University in Norfolk, Virginia. She then followed up with positions in Human Resources and Accounting before finally settling down into her current creative mode. When she's not writing, Sue spends her spare time playing tennis, gardening, and dabbling in technology.

www.ingramcontent.com/pod-product-compliance
Lightning Source LLC
Chambersburg PA
CBHW051801040426
42446CB00007B/463